365 DAYS OF TRANSPARENCY

365 DAYS OF TRANSPARENCY

DAPHANNY BAKER

J Merrill Publishing, Inc., Columbus 43207
www.JMerrill.pub

Copyright © 2021 J Merrill Publishing, Inc.
All rights reserved. No part of this publication may be reproduced, distributed, or transmitted in any form or by any means, including photocopying, recording, or other electronic or mechanical methods, without the prior written permission of the publisher, except in the case of brief quotations embodied in critical reviews and certain other noncommercial uses permitted by copyright law. For permission requests, contact J Merrill Publishing, Inc., 434 Hillpine Drive, Columbus, OH 43207
Published 2021

Library of Congress Control Number:
ISBN-13: 978-1-950719-92-1 (Paperback)
ISBN-13: 978-1-950719-91-4 (eBook)

Title: 365 Days Of Transparency
Author: Daphanny Baker

This book is dedicated to my God-Given mother, Alean Ramsey Porter for believing that I could do anything! Her favorite words were, "Peaches can do it!" I love and miss you dearly Mama and I THANK GOD for blessing me with you!! RIP

To the most talented beings on this earth: MY CHILDREN; Eryonna, Reyc'haun, Diamond, and Javier! Thank you guys for pushing me to take this planet by it's horns and making it a great one!

And lastly, my husband, Bishop Melvin T. Baker, my Pookie, my Superman. Thank you for seeing this project through with me to the very end with a thumbs up the entire way.

INTRODUCTION

DDB TRANSPARENCY

When I was in the ninth grade my teacher advised me that I should be a writer. I honestly didn't put too much thought into what he said until I began to experience life's lessons. In 2014 I began to post transparent and mind provoking thoughts that would drop on me daily like a ton of bricks. It was then that I came to know that this was the course that I should take. Over the years my daily inspirations filtered into transparent moments that people waited for me to publish. It was even said to me through those post, "Girl you need to write a book!" So here we are; My endeavor is that as you peruse through these pages, you are blessed immensely and that my candidness reaches you in a heartfelt expression. I extend to you my hand, I lend you my shoulder and I offer you words of encouragement right here in this book. Thank you for reading.

DAY 1

TRUSTING GOD IS ALL YOU NEED.

We will all go through storms; however, Trusting God gives you comfort throughout! Yes, it is great when God comes through in the 11th hour, but wouldn't it be great if we could rest easy knowing that God is already on the case.

Knowing that he will supply your needs, he's going to make a way of escape, and the weapon that is formed against me WILL NOT prosper, assures you that this won't last always. God is a God that keeps his promises, and if we could grasp that, it'll be a whole lot of trusting ~vs.~ too much worrying.

I'm here to remind you that while you're trying to figure it out, He's already worked it out!! #TrustHim

DAY 2

*L*ife can be something else at times, as well as the people in it.

I strive earnestly to love everyone and forgive those that have wronged me. This is a daily walk for me. And throughout the day, I often find myself whispering to God and asking for His divine help.

I don't want God to return, and I NOT be ready due to unforgiveness in my heart. What helps me is seeing people for who we ALL are, and that is Sinners saved by grace.

I do not have to be in their company; however, I do have to love and Forgive.

So, if you struggle with this (as I do), Remember that God forgives us, so it is important and commanded that we forgive others No matter how they trespass against us. #Forgive and Live!!

DAY 3

HAVE YOU EVER HAD A CONVERSATION?

...and right in the midst of talking, you realize something about yourself? I've realized that I do NOT judge individuals and worry about their business because there are areas in my own life that I need God to work in.

I was conversing with a close friend of mine yesterday and realized that I truly need God. Weights that I've carried that I need freedom from are resting on me.

Many are too busy scaling the area that they can't see that they're walking around with open wounds and unhealed scars. There is so much clean-up in your OWN house that you need to stay home and out of the window of others!

I thank God that he loves me enough to reveal me to ME!!! There is a danger in knowing everyone else and not even knowing YOU! Pointing the finger when three are pointing right back at you! Drop the scalpel, Ma'am / Sir, and work on your OWN self! #SurgeryInMotion

DAY 4

DO YOU EVER WISH THAT PEOPLE COULD SEE YOU FOR WHO YOU ARE?

So many have different views of you. One or two may be spot on, but then there are those individuals who have no clue what they are talking about.

I am a shy person, but if you ask an onlooker about me, they would probably say the complete opposite. It astonishes me that people will take the time to speak "on" you but will not take the time to get to know you factually! Can you relate to that?

Do people say things about you that you are wondering who the heck they are talking about? Learn a person before you speak on them. The eye sometimes deceives us. #TuneIn

DAY 5

HOW DO YOU FEEL ABOUT YOUR ENEMIES?

How do you treat them? Some people say they like to keep their enemies close  "NOT ME!!!" now I'll pray for them like the Bible has instructed. I'll even feed and give to 'em, if there's a need. But I definitely WILL NOT keep them in the boat with me.

Many situations in our lives arise because we have some individuals way too close that know things about us that only Jesus should. I am saying to you, watch who you have overeating your good fried chicken and showing your blueprints. They may be building your very house! #BE CAREFUL

DAY 6

WHAT DO YOU THINK OF YOURSELF? We can sit and write others' attributes all day, but what can you say about YOU? Often, we let people label us as being conceited if we say nice things about ourselves. But the truth of the matter is that there's nothing wrong with looking in the mirror and saying, "Girl/Man, you look amazing today!"

The problem is, we can give everyone else a compliment, everyone but ourselves. When someone gives you a compliment, you downplay it by saying something negative. JUST SAY THANK YOU!!

Start seeing your beauty too, love on yourself too, you build YOU up too! I LOVE ME start loving YOU too!

DAY 7

WHAT WERE YOU FEELING WHEN YOU WOKE UP? Did you "wake on the wrong side of the bed" Were your words, "Not today!!" or did you wake with a song in your heart and God on your mind?

My prayer is the last one for you. We really do determine the flow of our day; yes, the enemy may send something, but it doesn't have to infiltrate!! It may form, but it doesn't have to prosper. Tell the enemy about the God that you serve.

We'll often declare what the devil has done, and we fail to stand up and use the weapons that we were born with. (Born again) I admonish you to start your own day off. Don't let something or someone start it for you!

Make a conscious effort to wake up convinced that God is in control and "NO" weapon that is formed against me shall prosper today or any other day!!! You've Got This!!! NO WEAPON!!!!

DAY 8

WHAT INSPIRES YOU TO KEEP GOING? Life can be hard at times, and the truth is every one of us has asked, "what's next?"

Sometimes we fall, and instantly something tugs on us, or we'll lay there for a while, and just before that thing wipes us out, a hand reaches to pull you up! Whether it's your children or your faith, choose what inspires you to hold on and grip tight!

God will never put more on you than you can bear, and when things get too hard, he'll give you a way of escape. Trust the hand.

DAY 9

SOMETIMES, YOU MUST SEE WHAT GOD IS SAYING THROUGH IT ALL through the turmoil and the pain, we're not trusting God. We just want the uncomfortableness to stop.

I believe that there is a lesson to be gained in everything, no matter how Good or Bad the situation is. Start going through your storms with Grace ~vs.~ racing to get out of it. I promise you, there's a message in it.

When I lost my 1st daughter, as I reflect, there were a few things that I learned: (1) I really wasn't yet ready to be a mother then and (2) In years to come, the loss taught me to love, cherish and appreciate every moment with my family!

There is purpose in your pain. Walk it out, don't Run out! Learn something!!

DAY 10

GOD IS IN CONTROL of everything!! It may look bleak; you may have counted things out, but only God knows the end! Although the President is stalling, hoping to gain something, and looking stupid, AT LEAST he's hoping!

If you have to faith it or "STALL" it or call those things that Are not AS THOUGH THEY ALREADY ARE, you need to do that! Help is on the way. You must wait like you're waiting for it.

God sees, and he's aware. You just have to trust him! STALL THE COUNT!

DAY 11

INVEST in "YOU!" It is perfectly fine to see what someone else is worth but make sure that you don't shortchange yourself in the process.

As a church people, we are taught to bless others and sometimes at the stake of ourselves. I admonish you today to take yourself to the movies, treat yourself to dinner, splurge on **you** for once, don't always put YOUR stuff back at the register (I'm guilty of this). Continue to be a blessing to others. However, add a little YOU to the equation. The word tells us to love our neighbor as ourselves, so this must mean that you are to love yourself as well.

So, love on but don't forget about the person in the mirror.

DAY 12

I often make the statement, "**SINCE YOU'RE BREATHING,** you have time to make it right!"

In life, we WILL make mistakes, but the worst thing you can do is give up! Mercy is granted every morning, and as long as you have breath in your lungs, you can start over! Do not look at it as you keep failing.

Look at it as "This might be the time that I get it right!" One of the best decisions I've ever made in my life was to TRY AGAIN! The reason the enemy whispered in your ear that you cannot come back from this is that he knows the best is yet to come!! We just have to convince YOU of this.

Don't let your thinking errors rob you of what's next! Inhale, then exhale!! You're a decision away from your blessing!

DAY 13

What has God assigned to your hands, and what have you allowed to hinder your assignment?

Years ago, I allowed some very piercing words of an individual to hinder my daily inspiration. I allowed their words to creep into my spirit, which gave me writer's block!

So, I was "Not only" blocking my blessing, but blocking other's blessing. Different ones would ask for the daily inspiration, but I just couldn't bring myself to write.

I'm being transparent today to plead with you to never let anyone or anything prevent you from fulfilling your assignment! I went from writing every day to letting months lapse! You'll never know whom you're helping, so don't "YOU" let the enemy hurt your ministry!

If God gave you the torch, keep it lit! Ignore the distractions.

DAY 14

Are you prepared for what you're asking God for?

We have a laundry list of requests, but the truth of the matter is if God were to give you your heart's desires, YOU'RE probably NOT READY?

Asking God for a spouse and your attitude stinks, or a million dollars, and you can't even manage the $3 you have. You already make every excuse why you don't go to church. YOU'RE NOT READY!! Before you Petition, you need to prepare!!

Get your house in order before you invite others in.

DAY 15

What is it that you do when you feel pain, or you feel uncomfortable, or something is overwhelming you?

To be totally honest and transparent, mine "WAS" running! My favorite saying was always, "I don't Sit in Pain!" But the truth is sitting in pain or running from the pain is not what God has commissioned me to do! I realize that the only way to combat the pain, the discomfort, and/or the feeling overwhelmed is on my knees, asking God TO HELP ME! I was too busy defending MYSELF or comforting MYSELF or getting out from under the pain instead of blanketing all that with the shed blood of Christ! I can do all things "through Christ" … not running! I didn't accomplish anything by running but everything by trusting God!

Let Go and Let God!

DAY 16

So many have the word "Love" tangled.

Although I love gifts, love isn't about purchasing things. Although compliments are nice, love is not about admiring someone's appearance. Love isn't being around someone all day to feel their love. Love helps someone be the best they can be, taking them halfway and allowing them to learn the rest. Some may think if you tell them "No," you don't love them, but I can truthfully say that most of my greatest accomplishments have been birthed through hearing the word "NO!" I love you, so I won't enable you.

I'll teach you to do it for yourself!

DAY 17

Will you still serve God even in the midst of horrific obstacles?

A lot of conditions will evolve that will show you exactly where you are in your faith. Some things will cause you to fight, and some things will knock you down, and you will feel like you cannot go on.

When you are not prepared for a blow, at that moment, you'll see what you're truly made of. Will you take it on the chin and get back up, or will you lay there and be disqualified?!... I choose to fight back... and with everything within me, I am going to win! Don't let the cares of this world and the launching of heinous attacks swallow you up.

You were born to win!!

DAY 18

One may ask, "Where do the storms of life come from?" Are we reaping some things? Is it a certain time of life that you must experience this?

My husband reminded me of Job in the Bible. His storm wasn't self-induced. Yet, he endured it, and, in the end, he was notably rewarded! We may not want to go through some of the things that come upon us but on the other side of through is a great blessing "IF" you'd hold on! No one wants to experience the lows, but seemingly everyone wants to experience the highs.

Get this, some of the most prominent people have come from a valley or a back alley. If you keep the end in mind, you can go through with a smile.

Your now is not your later!

DAY 19

Getting to know new people is ever so hard nowadays because you don't know who to trust.

We build walls and protect the entry of our heart to avoid the inevitable pain and loss. But the truth of the matter is we may have kept ourselves from some of the most phenomenal alliances and non-blood relatives.

I'm not saying not to be careful because God knows I am. However, don't be too careful to "not" take risks. Life is short, and we must learn how to Love like God does. Seeing people through his eyes!

Seek God in every encounter and embrace the ones that are meant to be a part of your beautiful journey.

DAY 20

Going through can be a critical thing; you cry at the drop of a hat; you can become distant and isolate yourself from everyone. You May even feel like you're in this all alone because when you lean on someone, you feel like you're a burden to them and an annoyance. "THE MANY" times you shed a tear, get sad, or mention that person's name, now you are at the point of keeping it inside and just talking to yourself ONLY!

After a while, you will find yourself going through it "by yourself" just so you won't be viewed as weak or a whiner. A storm can be raging!! Full of rain, cold and hot times, but I know someone who has carried ME even when I didn't know I was still going, and here I STAND today! With my mind still intact, stronger, and much wiser.

You have to hold on even when you don't know what's next. YES, mistakes will be made, and you JUST might feel like giving up but HOLD ON to GOD!! I'm glad that I did.

DAY 21

Are Hard times really hard times? We go through things in life, and those things come to make us stronger, not to kill us.

Every experience should make you wiser for the next, and every ounce of pain should make you stronger and more prepared for the next blow. Don't look at every storm as life-threatening. Some tornados come to tear up the old so you can start anew!

Take an optimistic/Faith view. Things are not as bad as they look!

DAY 22

When you already know someone's M.O., don't even let what "THEY DO" affect you! Liars will lie, cheaters will cheat, thieves will steal, and haters will hate!! Idiots will be idiots, and Clowns needs an audience! Don't buy a ticket to the circus!! They'll try their darnedest to get you to participate, but don't you dare!!

What determines your level of maturity is how you handle or react to certain things. Some things need not be addressed, and every little thing doesn't require a response. As long as you continue to take the bait, they will continue to throw you the line.

Join the 3-monkey ministry - see, hear and speak no evil. And don't be easily provoked!

DAY 23

Because **this is one of the last few days in the "LOVE" month**, I just want to reflect. Love is one of the loudest words. You cry aloud because of it. You laugh loud because of it; you smile loud because of it. Your actions are even loud due to it! Love controls your everything!!

When you find it, you'll know it, because you won't be able to contain it!!

DAY 24

*H*ow you feel about yourself and treat yourself will show others how to treat and Feel about you! "YOU" Love on YOU. "YOU" get to know you. "YOU" have respect for YOU…which will Provoke others to follow suit! Get ahold of your "OWN" life so that others have no other choice but to come correct.

We have to stop receiving less than we deserve!! PERIOD!! Stay ready! So, they'll come into your life ready!

DAY 25

Masking the pain with something or someone is doing more damage to your situation because you're not healing. You're still hurting, but you don't know it because it's covered by the mask. Your mask could be denial, people, drugs, or alcohol.

Rip the masks off and expose that pain to the light. Allow yourself time to heal! #ItsForYourMaking

DAY 26

There comes a time in one's (My) life when we have to **Take responsibility for our own actions**. I've learned while going through life… when I make a decision, it's "my" decision!! No one forced me I made the decision, so the blame can't be put on anyone else if it turns out to be the most stupid and outlandish decision. If "by chance," I end up with someone that is totally not for me, it was totally my decision. If I go somewhere that's totally not for me, and something horrific happens, it was totally my decision. We have to stop blaming people for our actions!!

My actions, my consequences. Be wiser in your decision making.

DAY 27

*I*magine life without woes. How would one know how to appreciate life in its entirety? Although we don't like to experience suffering, pain, and/or losses, it's extremely uncomfortable. But it shows you that you're stronger than you thought. Take life as it comes and smile as you're coming through what "you thought" would kill you!!

You're a champ, and with the right gloves, you can fight your way out of ANYTHING!! Ding-Ding

DAY 28

You ever have a humbling experience that knocks you down but also wakes you up?! An experience that is devastating enough to catapult you in the Direction that was actually meant for you! One that makes you appreciate and look forward to life ahead... James said to count it all joy. Everything that I've endured has come to tweak me.

I cannot and will not complain because it ONLY gets better from here!! Watch this!!

DAY 29

Worrying frantically about what life will deal you next? Why? Don't accept what is offered to you. You slam YOUR list of demands down on the table! Stop letting people, places, and things determine what's next for you. Sit down and write a list of your S.M.A.R.T. goals (Specific, Measurable, Attainable, Realistic, and Timely). This is what we teach the youth at my Job and guess what, it's not too late for you to start!!

When you set your plan, you won't be waiting nervously on the plan.

DAY 30

*L*oving God is easy and trusting God is easy. It's our "own" selves sometimes that we don't love, trust, and respect. Learn how to love yourself enough that you won't "beg" for the love of others and trust yourself (your gut) enough that you won't settle for anything less than you deserve.

Sometimes you have to remind yourself to love and trust YOU!! And allow God to love you enough that you'll let him guide you.

DAY 31

Do you ever feel like a sitting duck? Like you're just prey, waiting for something to happen. And that no matter how good of a person you may be, bad things do happen to good people. Yes, there are some unfortunate and unforeseen events. But My bible says, after you've suffered awhile, the God of all grace will restore, strengthen and establish you. Sometimes your life will be ripped to shreds just so God can restore and re-establish you! Don't look at what just happened as a disaster. Count it all joy because God is getting ready to Prove to you "JUST" who he is AND right in the midst of the ones that hurt you!

Don't lose sight of the morning. It's almost daybreak!

DAY 32

I **will not allow the strength that "I ASKED" God for to weaken me.** When we ask God for strength, he doesn't just give us muscles. Nor is Strength going to just magically appear. We sometimes have to fight to get strong or push ourselves to gain resistance. You have to work for it; you must keep going! Stay in the race and run like you're in the finals. So that you may become effective.

Paul said in 1Cor 9:27 that, I discipline my body like an athlete, training it to do what it should. Otherwise, I fear that after preaching to others I myself might be disqualified.

DAY 33

Some parts of your journey will be rough and will almost seem as though it will wipe you out; And though you may stumble and fall, God is right there to see you through.

Trust God even through the difficult parts I know I am.

DAY 34

Once you've been shown/experienced "**TRUE**" **love,** you'll recognize all of the other counterfeit stuff. It's like purchasing an authentic Louie Vuitton. You'll be able to spot a knock-off right away.

Don't settle for less!

DAY 35

Storms are meant to trouble the waters; God is there to Calm them. When the enemy thought this would rock your world, you found out that as long as you held on to God, it actually turned out better than you thought.

Trust God. He'll give you peace in the middle of it.

DAY 36

*D*o You ever feel like you bent down to tie your shoe and stood up, and you were 49? You go through life accomplishing so much, yet still NOT being able to account for the Wasted years. What do you do with that? What do I do now? You might ask. You gather your thoughts, readjust your Tiara/Crown live out the rest of your life as though you are approaching the END of your life! Do not let the thought of wasted years hinder your future years!

You have MORE to do!! So, DO IT!!

DAY 37

You ever look at someone and want to ask, "What happened?" Or "**Who did it?**" A lot of Individuals are walking around with misplaced anger and unaddressed behaviors, making you want to almost go back in time with them and help them find out where things went wrong #SoSad.

DAY 38

Sometimes, to not become bitter or hate a person or people, you have to know when to **Cut ties and Walk Away**. Sometimes their season is over, but you try to force "what should've been A SEASON" into a lifetime! Pray and ask God what their position is.

DON'T let a Hot minute turn into Hate!

DAY 39

No one's testimony is the exact replica of someone else's. In fact, I don't desire or covet your testimony, and I'M SURE you don't want mine. I can't even fathom what you've been through, and you have no idea what I've been through.

Nonetheless, we sure can use what we've been through to help someone else get through!! Help someone overcome!

DAY 40

I do not get caught up in what others have **because I know what God has for me is for me,** and vice versa. God distributes to his children in ways that we could never understand! I like to affectionately refer to myself as "God's Favorite. Yet the truth is that he loves us all so much, and his word says, no good thing will he withhold from them that walk upright period!! I appreciate how God considers us.

Let's continue to stay in his Good graces so we can continue receiving his Choice blessings!

DAY 41

*D*o you ever just pause and ponder on the favor that is over your life? The ways made, the things that were prevented from happening to you, that way out, the underserved Blessings, etc. I often say, "favor isn't fair, but I like it!" Our lives are filled with so much unmerited partiality. And we aren't even conscious of it sometimes. Doors closed, doors opened, avoided relationships, new relationships, that new car or home, new Job…

God knows what's best, that's why his no is a no, and his yes is a yes trust His Favor and rejoice in it!!#DDB TRANSPARENCY

DAY 42

Stand up for who you are and what you believe in. It's okay to support someone else. However, you never want to lose yourself in someone else's path. People will try to guilt you into pouring all of your efforts into their dream box and will go as far as convincing you that you're not loyal if you try to step away; meanwhile, your aspirations are on the back burner, burning up!

Don't forfeit your dreams for someone else's. You have purpose too! You can help theirs but don't hinder yours!

DAY 43

What do people see when they look at you? Would the world be a better place if there were five or six more of you, or are people asking God what he was thinking? Are you living a peaceable life, or are you disturbing others' peace? We are here on Earth to make a difference and an impact, not to muddle or agitate humanity. Are you one who agitates or impacts?

Make your reputation a great one. It's the most important part of you.

DAY 44

Being who you are trumps who they are "Trying" to be, any day! No matter what goes on around you, stay true to you. Fads may change, seasons may change, people may even change. But do not alter YOU while others are all over the place.

Stay on YOUR course. What works for THEM may not work for YOU.

DAY 45

Don't let the hang-ups of others make you hang it up. Your path is not their path. So, don't allow others to dictate your direction. Sometimes people can be so controlling, yet their own lives are totally out of control. Stay on track, keep your focus, and press your own gears.

Live the journey that God has designed for YOU exclusively. Not others.

DAY 46

Small-minded and Carnal minded individuals will never understand God's big plans for your life!

Don't expect carnality to comprehend the spiritual.

DAY 47

Don't do what your flesh wants you to do. Do what God tells you to do.

With God, you win; with Flesh, you lose!!!

DAY 48

Don't tell me that God won't step in and keep you! I had an inkling to do something this week that Would have totally upset my walk. I'm so glad that God keeps his hedge of Protection around us! Although we feel like we're our own person, we're NOT! We were bought with a price, and one act or deed could Upset the whole thing! As I was driving to work this morning, "Secret Place" (Karen Clark-Sheard) came on my radio. My spirit man was immediately awakened, and I began to cry. God was letting me know that even when my enemies (that thing) come to consume me, he'd keep me safe from harm! He will hide you in his Tabernacle!

No matter what's going on around you, you stay in the safety of the master's arms.

DAY 49

*C*aring for your **inner man is just as you would care for a baby!!** You have to cherish it, feed it, clothe it, nurture it, tell it no, discipline it, guard it, and make sure it grows correctly! You can't allow just anything near it. You have to watch what it hears and watch what goes in and out of its mouth, and you have to keep a constant watch over it!

Are you a good parent, or do we need to contact CYS? Christ-Your-Savior.

DAY 50

I've been through some bitter times in my life, and I've also experienced awesome moments in which God Blew my socks off. However, I can honestly say that right now, at this very moment, I'm grateful for the state that I'm in at this point and time. God is dealing with my Inner man!!! It matters NOT if I have a thousand degrees or millions of dollars in the bank, and I still fail to make it in. I DON'T WANT TO BE LOST!!!

The most urgent thing for me right now is my soul!!! I need God to clean me up from the inside out before it's too late. Everything else can wait.

DAY 51

*T*he Blessing in it all is that God is RIGHT THERE!!

DAY 52

*L*ove yourself through the Good, the Bad, the Ugly, and EVERYTHING in between.

Stay true to yourself!!

DAY 53

Did you know that everyone is not going to like you?
No matter how nice you are, how cool you are, or how down to earth you are, someone will still hate your guts. I had to adopt the "I've got Jesus, and that's enough" song because people will have you fine-tuning yourself every other day to suit whatever bag they're coming out of that day! Don't get too comfortable with individuals because they're here today and gone tomorrow. They're with you one moment...But the moment you climb out of their web, they cease all dealings with you. They will even influence others to participate in the charade. Don't fret or get all alarmed. It is a disguised blessing because you don't need the foolishness in your life anyway.

Let 'em leave and count your blessings!

DAY 54

*L*ord, help me NOT be so focused on others' faults that I can't see MY OWN blunders!

DAY 55

*E*veryone will go through some hard times at some point. Life isn't always easy. Just something to think about. Did you know the people that are the strongest are generally the most sensitive? Did you know the people who exhibit the most kindness are the first to get taken advantage of? Were you aware that the ones who take care of others all the time are typically the ones who need it the most? Know this; 3 of the hardest things to say are I love you, I'm sorry, and please. Help me.

Sometimes a person may appear happy, but you may have to look past their smile to see the pain to help them. This thing "Called life" is very real!!

DAY 56

When a series of unexplained and unfortunate events happen in one's life, the question should be asked, "God, what is going on?" Sometimes it's a "Job experience," and sometimes, this individual is reaping the things he/she has put out. Do a Self-evaluation. If it's a Job experience, thank God for what's to come. If you're reaping, thank God because it wasn't what it could've been!!

Life is short. Monitor your output and your input.

DAY 57

*I*n life, some things will take you by surprise, and some things you just expect. Nonetheless, take either one and roll with the punches. Don't let either stunt your growth or keep you from moving forward.

Your progress is certainly Greater than your distractions. Keep going!!!

DAY 58

You may be placed into situations that look like it's going to tamper with your goal. However, with much willpower and unflinching determination, any impediment will be overcome. If you can just keep your mind affixed to the prize, NOTHING is unattainable!

Continue to vigorously make great strides to move forward. You will arrive at the finish line before you know it and with a sizable amount of joy.

DAY 59

Do you ever wonder how people live with themselves?

What level of consciousness they possess! Their secret indiscretions the things "THEY THINK" they are getting away with! "With you" but behind your back doing contrary to all they have committed unto you!! Don't worry, your pretty/handsome little head. They may be getting by, but "TRUST" they are NOT getting away! There are eyes in EVERY place that catches the faintest act! No one can harm you and get away with it!! This is what I hold to.

My God is always awake and has seen even that thing that one has erased!! Be encouraged I CERTAINLY AM!!

DAY 60

An individual that is never satisfied is not stable. They're here, they're there eating here, sleeping there, at this job this week and that job next week. They aren't giving a 100% to any one place, person, or thing! Without stability, there's confusion. Confusion breeds inconsistency, and inconsistency leads to a lack of commitment, which generates struggles.

One should Create a healthy, sane, and stable life. Whether it be over here or over there, just elect Permanence!

DAY 61

Whatever God Allows, I'll take it!! Sometimes you have to let go of what "you think" is GOD to receive what God really has for you!!

Let go and let God! And be willing to accept it! I'm ready!!

DAY 62

*D*o you ever feel like the men in your life failed you? From your Father, that should've been in your life and protected you, to your uncles, your brothers, and or every man that made you a host of promises in which none was fulfilled. There is ONE man that Always has and will definitely keep EVERY promise to you! He will even go as far as to NEVER ever turning his back on you, no matter how Arduous times get or how big of a mess you may create of your own life. He will supply your every need and comfort you in need.

You may not put your trust in any other man ever again, but this man you can CERTAINLY trust!! Trust GOD!!

DAY 63

When you're not whole, you'll find that you do things incomplete.

You can't fully give of yourself when you're not your whole self.

DAY 64

When you see someone in high stride trying to make BETTER of themselves, do you often hear people on the sidelines uttering these words? "She/he thinks they're better than me!" Personally, that is one of my greatest pet peeves because One would have no room to make that statement if they were real busy making moves themselves for the betterment of their own selves. I'm never concerned with someone trying to be better and do better because I'm over here doing what I do to make this "MY" best life! It's okay to compliment and admire someone else's accomplishments; however, don't get caught up in envy and compare your things with theirs because progress and success are attainable for ALL!! Achieve your goals and make your life your best life! Focus on being better today than you were yesterday.

Make this year better than Last year, and your now greater than your then!! Concentrate on YOURS!! NOT THEIRS!!!

DAY 65

Are you ever confused with your life? The way things are going, where you're at, the job you're working, whom you're with? Your plans and goals for yourself do not match your present path! This is not how you envisioned your life to turn out! You've begun to question God, question your steps, trace your steps, and wonder if this is it. Listen, I am here to encourage you to keep pushing!! As long as you're breathing, you can adapt, adjust, and ascend to the greater!

No one can stunt your growth except you!! Challenge Create and Charge!!

DAY 66

Are you afraid of what it "Looks like?" What my marriage "Looks like," what my finances "Look like," what my children "Look like," or what my spiritual life "Looks like!"? Things may look like one thing but actually, be something else. The enemy's job is to get you so focused on what it looks like that you lose sight of what it actually is. It looked like the woman with the issue of blood would always be in that state, and it looked like it was the end for Job, but he ended up with more than he initially started out with.

Stay focused and do not get discouraged about your NOW It's not what it looks like.

DAY 67

*I*n this whole round world, you may feel overwhelmed. Surrounded by a plethora of family, friends, folks on your job, and even people in your church! I've learned, you still have to find your inner peace! When you find that place in you that is still uninvolved with the cares of this world and full of life, you've found your "Peace Spot." In this chaotic world that's swallowed up with ferment and agitation, we desperately need a place that we can whisk off to swiftly.

Locate your inner peace and maintain the serene part of you so that you may preserve your sanity. We all need a safe house!

DAY 68

*D*id you ever look at someone and say to yourself, "Now that's a behavior I don't ever want to mimic?" One of my sayings is, "You are who you are, no matter where you are!" Meaning; I don't have to conform to my environment. When you were raised with morals and values, some things will be a stench in your nostrils. Don't be duped; being upstanding and Nobel when others choose not to screams sophistication!

Be someone that others hold in high regard -vs.- an atomic fool!

DAY 69

There is skill in knowing your worth. So many suffer from low self-esteem because they have no clue what makes them distinctive and amazing. When you find value in yourself, you will not accept anything less. You may not know who you are due to not spending enough time getting to know yourself. The key to tuning in to your worth is being alone with yourself and getting to know YOU exclusively!! When you gain knowledge of yourself, you will reject absolutely any opinions of others that have no idea who you are at all.

Learn how to spend time alone, you'll discover that you're not half bad company and you'll also find out some astonishing attributes about yourself.

DAY 70

Do you ever feel like you're mixed? I'm not referencing Caucasian and black or Puerto Rican and black. I'm talking about being where you are, but there's another part of you that's driving you to something GREATER! There's your natural side, but then there's the spiritual side of you that enhances everything about you! Your natural side is where your biological parents groomed you. But the spiritual side is where your heavenly father is perfecting you! Access your ancestry and gain knowledge of what lies in you!!

Don't just sow into your natural side but tap into your spiritual side, which brings you into a brand-new Vista of the "YOU" that your heavenly father created! BE GREAT!

DAY 71

In the midst of your life's story, you may ask? Where did he get this punchline, why did a loved one have to die, why couldn't we have stayed together, why did they have to scandalize my name? Etc. Well, you see, through every hurdle, you have gained strength in your legs to walk this thing out. Do not look at your situations as problems. Look at them as progress.

Praise God for your problems because your problems bring about your progress!

DAY 72

You may not understand your overwhelming days and nights, and you may encounter this or that; nonetheless, God is there to assure you that NO MATTER what you face, he has you! People may come and go. Yet, still, he remains. Keep your eyes on the prize and don't get distracted by the frivolous things.

Life is too short to concern yourself with anything other than what will guide you to your destiny.

DAY 73

Do you ever say to yourself, "I've got to stop allowing what people say define or deter me?" A lot of times, I'll say, "I don't care what people say!" But in the same breath, I find myself defending myself or hesitant to move forward the next time. People are opinionated, judgmental, and ignorant at times, but we (I) have to learn not to absorb others' critical cynicism. Jealousy will cause individuals to launch an attack on you. We are to protect and defend our minds and rid ourselves of any foolery quickly!

Be more focused on who you are and less focused on someone's opinion of you!

DAY 74

When you feel like you want to get out of character, STOP AND THINK. There is "NOTHING" more distasteful than allowing another to make you embarrass YOUR OWN SELF!! . Sure!!! Tit for Tat is fun; However, "Pure class" is knowing the art of restraint! Allow individuals to make a complete monkey of themselves. .BY THEMSELVES!! Wisdom is wise, So, when you get an inkling to retaliate. DO NOT!! It is so NOT worth the decline of your character, NOR will it benefit you in the climax of it all.

The Moral of this inspiration? DON'T BE EASILY PROVOKED!

DAY 75

Disagreeing with you is NOT arguing! Having my own opinion is NOT Arguing! Talking with my hands is NOT arguing! Having a discussion is NOT arguing! And Agreeing to disagree is NOT failed communication!

Don't force your opinion on the other person and just know that you will not agree on Everything. It's okay to "agree to disagree!"

DAY 76

The way you act determines where you're at!!

DAY 77

Sometimes the low road is the best road to take. The wrong road could lead you totally astray! In this life, we have to learn to follow the signs. Yellow using caution (being slow to speak or react), red stopping when necessary (Surrendering our will and or just shut up), and green continuing on (Keeping it pushing). Acts of recklessness can cause an accident that could potentially be fatal. Throw away "your" directions and use your GPS (God's Protected system)!

Yield to oncoming traffic. Meaning; humble yourself. There's a dreadful ending to always being on green!

DAY 78

*L*oyalty is something that should be held dearly!! When someone places their trust in your hand, your job is to protect it.

So many lose because they don't know the true value of anything!!

DAY 79

Nothing gives me more pleasure than being around **friends** and family whom I can be MYSELF with! In life's journey, you're in the company of all sorts of people, but being around people who have taken the time to know YOU is immeasurable.

DAY 80

I'm W-Willing, O-Optimistic, M-Motivating, A-Ambitious, and N-Nobel. I'm a Woman!!! I don't seek the affirmation of others. I don't suffer from low self-esteem.

I create my own path. I am A WOMAN!

DAY 81

Marriage is God-Lead, not Book-Read! We've endured some things that we wouldn't have made it if it had not been for God's leading.

Manuals are inspirational, but God has the Masterplan!

DAY 82

*L*ove is such an amazing thing. If one can merely grasp the true and exact meaning of love, we will not have so many misunderstandings, divorces, or losses. Love is urgent, and it's very much needed!

Explore the true meaning, then try it on. It'll bless your soul.

DAY 83

There is a **GREATER you inside of you.** Reach inside and pull out the Greater love, Greater success, and a Greater purpose. The only thing that can keep you contained is YOU!!

Strive for the best YOU.

DAY 84

Love Harder, Aim Higher, Go further but Say less! Don't always announce your dream; some things are better done on time than revealed early!

DAY 85

*L*ife can be as amazing as you allow it to be... Embrace your ups and downs as they come and strive for a greater "YOU" as often as you can!

Never settle for where you are; always set a goal to be Greater!

DAY 86

The whole journey was worth it!! Enjoy the sunshine, the rain, the bumps, the curves, the lows, the highs, the ins, the outs.

The whole journey will create the whole YOU!!! #DDB INSPIRATION#

DAY 87

Don't you think for one moment that you can play in the devil's playground and not get his dirt on your shoes.

Be careful where you go and where you play. You just may get dirty.

DAY 88

Do you ever find yourself wishing that you could run back in time and make sure "Right now" never happen? The truth is that regret can and will consume your mind and life if you let it! You must focus on making sure you're never at this point again.

As long as you are breathing, you can start again!! Make this next attempt count!!

DAY 89

Favor is such a beautiful thing that it picks out those that are not qualified and qualifies them. It grabs up those that don't have much and adds to their life equity. It also chooses the ones in the back and calls them to the front!

Favor isn't always fair, but it's a beautiful thing!

DAY 90

*L*ife is full of many challenges. Sometimes your greatest challenge is just waking up in the morning. But as long as you're waking up, you have the opportunity to turn your challenge into a change. Choose to use every obstacle to make you an overcomer and use every valley as a victory.

Life is already short; choose to go it wiser!

DAY 91

Waking up to a new day means a brand-new start, a brand-new outlook on life, and brand-new aspirations!!

Take advantage of this brand-new mercy that you were afforded and try things a brand "New" way.

DAY 92

Pressing forward may seem hard sometimes, and it may feel easier to just go back but keep going. Things are so much more rewarding up ahead.

DAY 93

What makes individuals act a certain way? Childish, silly, ignorant, etc. Is it their insecurities, past hurts, low self-esteem, and jealousy? Could it be because they're so miserable they want to see others miserable? It is so uncomfortable being in the midst of people who make the atmosphere tense and the room thick. There's nothing worse to me than "Grown folks" acting like juvenile delinquents. Sometimes you want to confront these individuals, but then that would make you just like them, huh? When will some adults grow up? Do they not know that once you turn a certain age, it's time out for life as it was on the playground at recess? We should be done with the whispers and the gathering of 4 and 5 friends to gang up on "One" person. It worries me to no end when a person needs an audience for his/her circus. If you're that good, then you should be a class act all by yourself!!

The moral of this inspiration - don't participate in someone's show if it is to kill another! Let them make a monkey of themselves BY THEMSELVES!!

DAY 94

*D*o you know of someone that has a sense of entitlement? Or are you that person? One that thinks that they have a right to everything they come in contact with. Even if someone else is in possession of it. Someone else's spouse, their home, their job, their money. The list can go on and on. You might've contributed one lyric to a song being written. Now you feel that you "deserve" ALL of the monetary return. Just because your niece spent one night at your house, you now feel that you should be able to file them on your taxes. Just because Your homie hit the lottery, it doesn't mean he has to give you one unearned cent! Life is not indebted to you!!!

Sit down and stop licking your chops at someone else's valuables, territory, and/or gain. THEY'RE NOT YOURS, and you're NOT entitled to 'em, PERIOD!

DAY 95

*L*ove, Joy, and Peace! 3 fundamentals of a fantastic life! Be driven to smile!!

DAY 96

"**LIFE" is filled with all sorts of surprises;** Good, Bad, Sad, Exciting, etc., etc. In the midst of it all, we have to stay in the "Master's hands." When things are "Good," we pray less; when things are "Bad," you can't beat us praying; when things are "Sad," we depend on others' prayers, and when things are "Exciting," we forget to pray. We are living in times where Prayer is "Key." And no matter what, it behooves us to Acknowledge God and Declare to the world that he is our source!! The Government would have us believe that their funds are our sustaining factor, but the truth is the cattle on a thousand hills belong to our savior. So, "I'll look to the hills for 300 Alex!"

Plug into the source and stay connected!

DAY 97

When you're comfortable in your own skin, you can be comfortable Anywhere, Anytime, and in the presence of Anyone! Love the "You" that God created!

Nobody can be you but you!!

DAY 98

What is life if you won't live it, what is love if you won't give it, what are dreams if you won't Pursue them, what are opportunities if you won't take them? Until you start to live, you're JUST existing. Until you start to demonstrate love, it's JUST a word until you put your dreams in motion. You're STILL asleep, and until you seize opportune moments, you're STILL missing it!

Take charge of your own life. The tools are in your belt, STRAP UP and Use them! #DDB INSPIRATION#

DAY 99

*S*ometimes when you have a moment, whether it be to cry, throw something or kick yourself, you have to do it in silence. Especially if you have people around that will judge you or plain ole NOT understand! In this Christian walk, amidst your trials, you will need to process all kinds of emotions, and a lot of the time, folks are not patient enough. They don't care enough and or are not equipped enough to help you! If I needed to burst out in tears, a wise woman once told me to do it during worship. This can be two-fold; 1. You can touch God. and 2. You can save face with people!!

Have your moment, but sometimes do it in Worship. #DDB INSPIRATION#

DAY 100

Life is a journey; take it in stride. There will be sweet days, and there will be bitter days. We just have to learn how to take the bitter with the sweet. Don't rush your journey, don't alter your journey, and please don't abort your journey! Take a stroll through the valleys, on the mountain top, and down the path of the unknown.

You may not see it now, but in the end, you'll realize that you had to take "that turn" to get HERE!! Keep Going!

DAY 101

Why do we as individuals settle for less? We're impatient. We think what WE WANT is NOT obtainable, or it's a temporary fix. Stop wasting time on things that will not keep your interest or match your dreams and aspirations!

Wait and choose wisely. You'll save yourself a whole lot of trouble!!

DAY 102

Husbands and wives ought to pray before seeking the advice of or soliciting the ear of others. In RARE instances, you find good council. In other instances, people 1. "Want your man" or 2. Are miserable because they don't have one.

"WE" need to be ever so careful of divulging the most intimate details of our marriages! Some we may call FRIEND, just very well may turn out to be a FOE!! #DDB TRANSPARENCY

DAY 103

When you're free, don't go back!! When the way of escape has been made, run like the dickens.

DAY 104

*I*n the END, the major thing was actually a minor thing!!
God is a heavyweight for your lightweight situations!!

DAY 105

Do not talk yourself out of what God has Already declared over your life!! #Wealth #Health #Happiness if God said it, HANG ON TO IT!!! No matter what it looks like at the moment!

DAY 106

Some things may not be easy, but they're certainly Doable!! Moving forward, going back to school, single parenting, starting a business, etc., through your eyes, it seems impossible. But with God's help, all things are possible!! What is not easy for you is an opportunity for God.

Give your hard tasks to a Man that can "DO IT EASILY!"

DAY 107

Are you thankful for life? Even if things aren't the way you'd like them to be, you're breathing, and SINCE you're breathing, you might as well be Grateful!

Embrace what is relevant and shun what isn't!!

DAY 108

Do things differently to get different results. If you are not pleased with your current situation, switch up, rearrange some things, and alter some of YOUR plans!

Change directions and monitor your surroundings. Change sometimes makes ALL the difference!

DAY 109

Don't **fight a battle that is not yours to fight.** Some things are way bigger than you.

Give it to that someone who will win EVERY fight, EVERY time!!

DAY 110

Through the good, bad, ups, and the downs; during the highs, lows, storms, and rainbows - you're yet making it through! You are built to last NO MATTER what day it is!!

DAY 111

When you think about living, what is the first thing that comes to mind? When you think about love, who is the first person that comes to mind? When you think about the pain you've endured, where is the first place that you reflect back to in your mind? Whatever, whoever, and wherever you may take your mental flight, God is life. God loves you best, and God has kept you through it all.

Anchor up in JESUS. He won't fail you, and he'll be with you through it all!!#DDB INSPIRATION#

DAY 112

*L***et LOVE drive you!** Keep yourself in the company of lovable people, practice doing lovable things, and let the WORD love roll off your lips "MORE" often.

Love is a beautiful thing when used properly! Drive it straight into someone's heart. No curves or deviations!

DAY 113

*L*ooking back in time, life can be so full of regrets. You might say, I didn't get enough schooling, I stayed in the world a little too long, I hate that I married whom I'm married to, I should've gotten it right with Aunt Mary before she passed, I shouldn't have had those drinks last night. We could sit and ponder all day. On all the things "We hate" that we ourselves created. But the fact remains. We cannot change the err of our Past. Will reflecting fix this hangover? Uh, That's a big fat NO! We have to accept yesterday for just what it is, "YESTERDAY!" Yes, we ALL have regrets. However, don't let the disappointment cause you a decline in life .use your memory of it to correct the next potential downfall. Declare to yourself that the next few choices have to be chosen cautiously and with a great deal of thought because I don't want to revisit this moment of regrets. We cannot change what we did last summer, but we can certainly prep for next June.

Start saving money, work on increasing your credit score, stop looking for a mate and let God send you one, etc., etc. Start Making your past worth reflecting on!! And with a Smile!

DAY 114

You don't need someone that will agree with your every decision, but you "DO" need some people to be loyal throughout the decisions you make! You'll know who's true by the decisions you make.

DAY 115

Rest your nerves, relax your mind. Change is just around the way. Things will get better, and before you know it, you'll be wondering when the change took place exactly! Focus on something else and occupy your time. You'll see, it'll turn around! A bleeding wound eventually stops, and a spill eventually dries up.

Keep going moving forward and let time work on your behalf.

DAY 116

No matter how hard you try to hold on, some people aren't meant to go any further with you! They've served their purpose. We mess up things by prolonging things and relationships that were supposed to end a long time ago.

Don't get mad or sad, Just Let them Go so you can Grow!

DAY 117

Love is absolute, flawless, beautiful, amazing, serene, sacred, fun, silly, honest, true, and many other great things if connected with the right person! It's an atomic explosion, and some people only get one chance at it! Enjoy!!

DAY 118

You can reflect, but don't regret! That was then, and this is now what didn't wipe you out, boosted you up! You now have a BETTER view; you can see things more clearly, and you definitely know how to keep your eyes open! Don't be upset. You needed that for what's to come! Be glad it happened because NOW YA KNOW!!

DAY 119

Be Thankful for your life and the ones in it! Tomorrow isn't promised to any of us. So, live today as though it were your last!

DAY 120

When You Love Someone, It's to your Benefit. You're doing what's commanded of you; you're mimicking Christ. We have to learn to stop loving with our hand out!!

Love with a Declaration, not an Expectation!!!

DAY 121

In all hurt, pain, and anger, there is a healing process. So many have gone straight into other relationships right fresh out of bad situations. Yes, "WE" get lonely, but we will do ourselves and others more harm than good without the proper healing.

Let's take the time to mend, regroup, and be restored. Things go so much better when we're WHOLE.

DAY 122

Did you know what you were going to be when you grew up? Did you declare who you would marry, where you'd live, where you'd work? Things don't always turn out the way we'd planned, but it goes all according to God's divine plan!!

Go with the Flow!

DAY 123

Life can be everything except mundane. As a matter of fact, it's a circus, roller coaster ride, and hurricane all rolled up into one, but when it's good, it's awesome! We won't harp on the lions, tigers, and bears because the sunshine, rainbow, and pot of gold certainly outweigh everything else.

Hang on during the storm. You'll be smiling again.

DAY 124

Society says we should do things this way and that way, we should eat this and not eat that. We should wear this and not wear that, be this size or exercise. We have to learn to be whom God created. A lot of people are doing this to their bodies, getting nose and boob jobs, because "society" says it's the going thing, losing a tremendous amount of weight that doesn't even suit you. Being you is the most popular person that you can be!

Love yourself. No filter or Altering needed!!

DAY 125

Y**ou've got to be determined to live on purpose,** out loud and in surround sound! Don't let anything or anyone distract you from living, laughing, and loving.

Life is too short not to enjoy it. Run, jump, dance, sing, and do it big!!

DAY 126

Use past lessons to help you ace the ones to come. Learn something from every round to stay on task. You don't want to have to repeat anything. Take in all you can. Something similar may be in the next round, but you'll be prepared because you learned all you needed last time. Life is a cycle.

You'll have ups, you'll have downs, just stay on track, and don't get stagnant!!

DAY 127

***S*omethings are good for you to go through if the lesson is learned correctly.** It makes you prepared for the next thing. Now you're searching for the signs that you overlooked the first time, you will ask the questions that you avoided the first time, and you will go in with your eyes wide open this time because of it! Your trial won't stop you from trying; it will just train you for the next one!

Go through and Grow You!!

DAY 128

I don't know about you, but when I'm done with someone, I'm done I don't do drive-by's., I don't stalk their social media, I don't ask anyone about them, I don't want anyone to keep me informed about them, I don't position myself to bump into them, I don't dress up so they can miss what they had, I don't keep in touch with their friends and family for the purpose of staying connected, etc. When you are done, YOU SHOULD BE DONE!!

Sometimes you gotta break all ties so you can heal, release, and move on! Too many games…someone will get hurt!

DAY 129

Don't get mad if I ask around about you, just as I wouldn't be upset if you inquired about me. Yes, I need to get to know you for myself and for yourself, so this is all a part of the process. You might have left something out, or I may be so engulfed "IN YOU" that I forget a few pertinent details that are very vital to our moving forward. A lot of people jump feet first into something and don't think to use their head at all. THINK people he or she has a "Before You!" You're Not necessarily holding them to their past but finding out some things from their past just might save your future!

Get enlightened, slow down and get to know him/her! I promise you, you will be glad you did!

DAY 130

You cannot reach for "Tomorrow" if you are holding on to "Yesterday!!" Drop it and move forward!

DAY 131

Don't get mad when people from your past do dumb stuff. It is just a friendly reminder of why you stopped fooling with them in the first place.

Just thank God!!

DAY 132

People do some homework! "MEN:" If every man before you was light complected and you're black as tar, ask questions! "LADIES:" If every woman before you was tall and slender and you're short and thick, inquire about his change of preference. Did they now get older/mature, and a certain look is no longer pressing, or am I just a temporary flesh move? You may be thinking long term. While in their head, you're just a fix until their future comes along, and the whole time they are looking at you like uugghh, Why am I with him/her?! Inquire!!

DAY 133

Why do we harbor ill feelings towards others? Life is too short to carry hate, envy, and strife around in our hearts! Forgive quickly, don't be so easily offended, and stop taking everything to heart. When we realize that "we" ourselves are not perfect, it will be easier to understand that mistakes will be made, people are going to do dumb stuff. They will err not once, not twice but a few times, and guess what, if you ask the people around you, you have too! So, lighten up, live, and let live and please let bygones be bygones!

Life is not promised!

DAY 134

You can't change the past and control what you should've or shouldn't have done, but you can change the present and future on what you will do and will not do!!

DAY 135

God will allow us to be thrown into the fiery furnace just so the onlookers can watch us come out unscathed, untouched, and in our right minds!

DAY 136

You can't tell your heart who to love. You can't beg, bribe, or beat your heart to STOP Loving someone! People may hurt you, betray you, even steal from you. But if you REALLY and truly love them, no situation, circumstance, or mishap will change your love! Love is a beautiful thing! Let's just hope it's reciprocated because it's awful to love hard and not "GET" loved hard!!

DAY 137

Let go of bitterness and Strife. It eats away at you like cancer!! Free yourself and Live!!

DAY 138

It is a great day to be alive. So many didn't make it to this point! You may not have all you want, you may not be where you want, but you are breathing! Life is short. The devil tried so many times to prevent you from seeing this day, but God blocked it.

Enjoy your brand-new mercy!!

DAY 139

There are three sides to every story your side, their side, and the truth! His side can be hyped up. Her side could have holes in it...but God knows the actual events.

DAY 140

Tearing others down won't build you up! Finding joy in another person's downfalls really speaks volumes about your own character. If they've wronged you, leave them to a God with a vengeance. He can and will repay far better than your miniature acts.

Stand down and watch God fight on your behalf!

DAY 141

These days are going like hotcakes! What are you doing with yours?

DAY 142

So many emotions - upset, worry, sad, mad, ashamed, confused. But there's only ONE that should be dominant, "HAPPY!" God has it all in control, no matter what it looks like. Good has already been determined to be the final outcome.

Take it in stride, take it on the chin, go to bed and wake up smiling. You're already the victor!!! JUST WALK IN IT!

DAY 143

Where are you now? Are you where you said you'd be? Growing up, we set goals for ourselves. We had a timeline of where we'd be at age 20, how many degrees we'd acquire by age 25, I'll be financially set by age 35, and so forth and so on! Are you there yet? You see, we made all these plans, but God had other plans. Although it may seem that you're way off course, you're actually right where you should be! You wouldn't have ever placed all these stumbling blocks along your way. You didn't plan to cry these many tears. But just to let you know, every obstacle, every sad day, every hiccup was orchestrated and all apart of "GOD'S" divine plan! I know you planned it another way, but you didn't create yourself. So you had no rights to your story!

The one that gave you life had plans "for your life," and you are right on task!!!

DAY 144

*E*veryone has an opinion but be careful that you don't force your opinion onto others. Just because blue is my favorite color, it doesn't make it the best color in the box. Just because you don't like liver, it doesn't make it nasty. Your beliefs are your beliefs, and my choices are my choices! Do things your way and let them do things their way. There is no wrong or right way to get somewhere, one set of directions may be longer than the others, but both directions will get you there.

You be you and let me be me. That's why God made you, you and me, me!!! And please Remember This when you're saying, "Child, if I were you!!" YOU'RE NOT ME!!!!

DAY 145

Who do you blame when things are bad? Who gets the credit when things are great!? When life is in turmoil, it's this One's fault, and "If so and so wouldn't have come into my life!" But when you're up and sitting pretty, your chest is stuck out, and "we" can't tell you nothing! News flash NOTHING happens unless God allows it. Good, bad, great, or indifferent. This life is not steady, there are going to be ups, and there will be downs. But in the midst of all the challenges and changes, you have to trust God to keep your mind intact! When you realize that this is all a part of the plan to develop and grow you, you'll flow accordingly.

We don't serve an up and down God. He will, however, certainly be there to lead and guide you. Hang on.

DAY 146

Do you know that you will make mistakes? Someone somewhere is beating up on themselves because they thought they were perfect. Someone somewhere is mad at their mate because he/she erred. The relationship was supposed to be perfect. Someone busted up a great friendship because they don't know that people make mistakes. No one is perfect, and everyone makes mistakes! When we all understand that, we won't be so eager to throw folks away. Outside of lying, cheating, and stealing (those are choices), people will break things, crash cars, and NOT pay you back on time… don't lose out on someone great because of a mistake!!

DAY 147

When you realize who you are, you won't allow anyone to tell you otherwise! You're not dumb; you're intelligent. You're not fat; you're fabulous. You're not "just" alright; you're amazing! Don't let the insults of others cause you to doubt yourself or look down on yourself!

Know your worth and accept Nothing less!

DAY 148

Float like a butterfly, sting like a bee! ~Muhammad Ali~
Do what you were created for!! Don't go through life without making your dent. If you sing, be known as a Psalmist; if you draw, be known as an artist; if you write, be known as prolific. Make your wings fly and make your stinger sting! Don't be just a church band; go out as an Orchestra! Make your mark! Leave your legacy! Don't close your eyes until you are named "Great!" You were not created to be just mentioned.

You were designed to be iconic!! Give your all and when you leave this earth, LEAVE YOUR NAME!!

DAY 149

Get to the place where you're comfortable with the skin you're in. Be free to love and be yourself! So many are walking around with baggy clothes, hats over their eyes, or just staying home even... because they're ashamed of what they look like. God created you, and whether you're darker complected, slightly bigger than the average model, a pimple or two on your face, or haven't received as many compliments as the girl/boy next door, you can still tap into what makes "you" outwardly appeasing! Who defines beauty anyway?

Do not base your looks on someone else's measuring stick! Be bold, be brave, and be beautiful!! COME OUT!!

DAY 150

Take life one day at a time... Guess what? You made it through yesterday, and today didn't come until today. No matter how miserable it was, yesterday was yesterday until 11:59, and it had to run its course. Today is yet another 24 hrs. So, since you're breathing, dot your i's, cross your t's, right your wrongs and forgive!! Tomorrow isn't promised to any of us, so live today like it could be your last day! Don't dwell on the past... fix what you can and leave the rest up to God!

Don't kill yourself over things that are out of your reach. Cry your cry, smile your smile, say your say, dance your dance and live your life!! YOU ONLY GET ONE!!

DAY 151

Domestic violence is real!! My heart and prayers go out to the women/men facing such violence. Many remain in situations because they feel there's no way out...whether there is some financial or emotional excuse! Some may say, "this isn't Domestic violence; he/she only shoved me. I was only hit one time, or maybe I upset them. This is why it happened!" Domestic violence is wrong and has claimed so many lives. It's not cute!! It's not love!! It's against the law!! The first strike could be the Last Strike!!

DAY 152

NEVER make a decision out of desperation, loneliness, anger, or grief! Never go shopping when you're hungry and watch what you say and do in the heat of the moment! Many of the things that we end up with or situations we find ourselves in, we look back and ask, "What the heck was I thinking?" Or "Why didn't I think that through?" Because we made decisions in the wrong frame of mind. Before you commit...ask yourself a bunch of questions.

You just may save yourself a great deal of money, stress, and wasted time. Hasty decisions can make or break us. So, please, be mo' careful!!

DAY 153

Grab a hold on your life. Don't let it take ahold of you!! Many are being tossed and shoved by a great storm. I say brace yourself for the next huge wind, and don't let it take you down!!

DAY 154

*I*f it didn't work "last time," take a different approach "THIS TIME!!" #But please don't give up!?!

DAY 155

What is your next move? Who does it involve? What does it entail? Is it positive? Who will benefit from it? Who will be affected by this? Does it require a lot of money? Is it feasible to do at this juncture?

Most importantly, have you consulted God? A lot of times, we move in haste; other times, we drag our feet. We have to learn to move in God's timing. One wrong, early, or late move can totally mess things up. Be cautious about being overzealous. Be careful about "waiting until you're financially set" or be cautious about mimicking someone else's moved.

Life is all about making moves. Just make sure your next move is the best move!!

DAY 156

Let's talk about "Trust" this morning. Trust can be broken in a matter of seconds, but it can take up to a lifetime to restore. Now I did say, "up to" because with the correct measures, the right motives and the greatest efforts are accomplishable! When someone's trust is broken, all they see is that hurt. Trust is a beautiful thing in a relationship "oh, but when it's broken!" You have no peace without it. There's always some form of breakout without it. Things don't function well, "without it!" Be careful of the actions you take and the decisions you make.

Contrary to popular belief, trust is needed in every situation, whether in your Christian walk, in marriage, amongst coworkers, between besties, or amidst a group that has concocted a plan to rob a bank!!!

Trust is vitally important! Consider the outcome of your next move!

DAY 157

It's hot, it's cold, this hurt, it's raining, I'm broke. We hear various complaints on a daily basis. We need one to see the other. The opposite of rain is a sunshiny day. The opposite of broke is having a pocket full of money! I couldn't fully appreciate a refrigerator full of groceries if I hadn't been hungry.

Take the good with the bad…it goes together, and it works together. Look at the BIG picture; it won't always be bad!

DAY 158

I won't give you a sad story. I'll refer you to a God that sits high, looks low, and SEE'S Everything!!! NOTHING gets by him, and I take comfort in knowing that no sin will go unpunished! I don't have to lift one finger.

He already knows how he's going to repay. Just get out of the way!!

DAY 159

Don't let anyone define your character. You'll find that it's the people that have known you the least amount of time that THINK they can tell you the MOST about you!! If we haven't experienced the good, the bad, and some things in between, you can't speak on my behalf. You can't introduce me to a crowd, and you certainly can't defend me against my haters. What's my demeanor during a crisis? Don't worry, I'll wait. What is my greatest joy on earth? I'm waiting EXACTLY!!

Don't let the rumor mill tell you who you are... let God show them exactly who you are!!

DAY 160

There's almost always someone that you can put ahead of yourself, someone that you'd say I don't want to see them hurt even if it's at your own expense. Sometimes...no "a lot of the times" you need to choose "You!" People will hurt you over and over again and expect you not to say ouch! You can be a victim for years, but when you decide to fight back, others don't understand why? Because you've allowed it for so long! Never give anyone an explanation as to why you decided to put "YOU" first! So many have died for others, gone to jail for the sake of others, and stayed in pain because they did not want to see someone else hurt!! STOP IT!!! Let every man/woman bear their OWN burdens.

Christ already died on the cross for man's sins. IT'S NOT YOUR JOB!! Enough is Enough! If They can dish it, let 'em eat it!!!

DAY 161

Who in your life supports your endeavors? Who is in your corner all the way? (Can you think of at least one or two) If you have just a couple of people who will stick with you, you can go a long way. This can be a lonely walk at times, but if you grab the hand of a friend and run... It's like having a gang. I hear people sometimes saying, "I don't need nobody!" But I assure you, EVERYBODY needs somebody!

Do not dismiss everyone; keep one or two great friends around ."TRUST ME" I wouldn't have gotten through half my trials without mine!!

DAY 162

*E*ncourage yourself even when things look discouraging. Tell yourself it's going to be alright even if it doesn't look like it, pull yourself together even when you feel like you're falling apart. Don't let trials get the best of you.

Hang on tight through the bumps, the bruises, and the storms. You can make it if you just hang on!!

DAY 163

In all things, you must become spiritual. Because carnality will lead you astray!!

DAY 164

Have you ever been so fired up and ready to Go for the Lord, then a situation occurs and Knocks you down to your knees?! Well, I say, since you're down there, Assume the position... It is time to pray! The enemy heard your declaration and took aim. He hit you, but he did not kill you.

GET UP!! #The Lord allowed it; don't embarrass him!!

DAY 165

When your life feels like you've missed your bus in inclement weather, remember this; It may get dark, you may be out there alone, and it may rain, sleet or hail even.

But don't give up, another bus is coming, and the bad weather won't last forever!!

DAY 166

od's Grace and Mercy prolongs your life. His love adds years to your life!

DAY 167

Cherish life and family like they're both going out of style!!

DAY 168

When going through tests and trials, you must know there is something to be learned. Even IF you don't understand the curriculum.

DAY 169

Repeat this prayer Lord, let my words and my actions exemplify you. Take out the "old me" and insert the "YOU me" Amen.

DAY 170

*I*t's a new day!!!

DAY 171

Who/What controls or determines your joy? Have you laughed uncontrollably lately? Is there a limit to your happiness each day? Everything goes better with a smile and a little chuckle. Have you ever laughed so long that people were anxious for you to stop to tell them what was so humorous? Continue to laugh even when people think you should be crying! Don't just show teeth to the dentist...

Show those pearly whites off on a regular basis! You're on candid camera!!

DAY 172

If you are ready to throw in the towel EVERY day and someone is always doing something to you. You need to check your surroundings and the people that surround you. We need people around us that will encourage, build, and challenge us - NOT ones that will drag us down and keep their foot on our neck. IF you're complaining all the time, that just means you want and need something to complain about. Otherwise, you'd get tired and do something about it!!

Stop giving individuals the power to ruin your day!#Have a Great Day on purpose the way God intended!!!

DAY 173

Imagine life without (What we call) the necessities - transportation, running water, phones, etc. We have become so dependent on things that some people have never even experienced!

Take a moment to be grateful for your needs "AND YOUR WANTS!"

DAY 174

Don't get your panties in a bunch because someone doesn't like you. There will always be that someone who will adore you! A lot of times, we miss out on the truest of love because we are so focused on certain ones that mean us absolutely NO GOOD! Focus on the ones that are loving you/on you, and you will not waste your time wondering who doesn't!!

Life is too short, don't be consumed with the foolishness of fools!

DAY 175

The person who seemed so unbreakable, breaks. The person who always seems to be laughing, cries sometimes. The person who seems so strong, may crumble. The person who seems to never quit, gives up 99 times in their mind is this you? Or will you still stand in the midst of it ALL?? Food for thought.

DAY 176

Are you counting down the minutes, hours, days, or months until something? Is it a good something? Or are you anticipating time up out of an unpleasant something? At any rate, in the meantime, I admonish you to love, live, laugh, and learn!!

Loving takes your mind off the time, living keeps you going, laughing makes things pleasant during that time, and learning keeps your mind sharp. In every situation, get something from it that will help you during the next situation!

DAY 177

Ladies: What are you worth? If you could and would put a price tag on your head, what would you say your true value is? Are you up there with Prada or down there with Payless! others will never know your worth if you keep going "ON SALE!" Keep the "Saks Fifth Avenue" mentality; someone somewhere will recognize your true value! If someone feels that you're too expensive, he's not the one.

Stay on the market until the right one comes along and is ready for his great investment.

DAY 178

What's your attire for today? Is it "dressed for Success" with a suit, a nice dress, casual slacks, and a nice pair of pumps? Or is it "dressed for less" with leggings, Walmart PJs, a headscarf, and flip flops? What statement are you making when you leave your house? Will someone notice you or nod at you? (True story) I know someone that got considered and hired for a BANK JOB just by her attire at the nail salon. You never know what today is.

Come out ready for Greatness!! Ya just never know!

DAY 179

Perhaps life didn't turn out how you'd planned—your career, your love life, your children, your Christianity, etc. One good thing, though, if you're reading this, you at least have one good breath to carry some things out. Don't waste your thoughts on coulda-shoulda-woulda's.

Get out there and make some moves! Life isn't over until it's over!

DAY 180

*L*oving someone beyond words is true art!! Loving yourself beyond words is a must!! They both require skill!

DAY 181

Keep things in perspective, don't lose focus. All sorts of things will come to distract you. Keep your eye on your goal, don't let issues and circumstances deter you from what you woke up this morning planning to do. Whether you have to walk or bum a ride, keep it moving!

Stay on the path, watch the signs, and look out for ditches! You'll get there if you just keep going!!

DAY 182

Anytime, Anywhere & in the presence of Anyone!! Make it a great day!! You be the positive atmosphere changer!!

DAY 183

There's nothing like being free!! Don't be bound up by people, places, or things!! Take off the shackles and soar!!

DAY 184

*L*ive today as though tomorrow isn't coming!!

DAY 185

What is greater than love? What is more promising than faith? What is more sacred than a vow? Life is full of so many things. However, some things just can't be tainted. Tampered with, yes. But not tainted!! Maintain the pure things.

DAY 186

There are always certain things that will bring people together. Whether it be weddings, births, tragedy, or reunions. You learn the magnitude of people's love in times like these. Is this a conditional love, or is it just plain ole' love proven? Some people say, "You only call me when you need me!" Others may say, "I call YOU 'because' I can count on you!" Tomato or Tomâto. It's all in how we look at it. Through situations, we have no idea what God is doing. The bible said he uses the foolish thing to confound the wise, meaning he'll use something that makes absolutely no sense to us. So, with the mending and coming together, nobody could have done that but God!! Before this, you weren't speaking to cousin Boo. Before that, Jack and Jill were planning a divorce.

Never underestimate the power of God's love and the things he uses to show his love. It's amazing!!

DAY 187

Respect begets Respect, trust begets trust, but "LOVE" is unconditional! You don't have to love me for me to love you.

The truth is, you can't tell your heart who and when to love.

DAY 188

What drives you to do what you do? Is it greed, selfishness, love, pride, faith, or your relationship with God?! Some of us go above and beyond to do certain things. Whether it be positive or negative, a whole lot of emphasis is put on your actions. Let what you strive for be named amongst others!

If you're going to work hard, let it be talked about, NOT laughed at in the days to come! Keep a positive status!!!

DAY 189

𝓗ope, Faith, trust, and Love!! Items of necessity check your bag to see what you're missing!

DAY 190

"True love" is an acceptance of all that is, has been, will be, and will not be

DAY 191

What will you Exchange? What can be replaced? What is worth giving up? And what can't you see your life without? Take a moment to comb through your life presently. If you're happy and you know it, say amen. If there's work to be done, Get to it! Live your life with a smile, no regrets, and less complaining.

Keep what's valuable, tweak what's fixable, and junk the trash. Enhance and Maintain your existence!

DAY 192

If you were getting scored on life, how close would you come to a hundred? Your promptness, your loyalty, your word, your faithfulness, your diligence, your love, etc. I mean, no one is perfect. Nonetheless, there's a degree of standard that everyone should hold themselves to. Sure, you can say what others are not doing. But what about you? When will it cease from being everyone else? When will you score big on your own efforts?

Take the measuring tape out and see where "YOU'RE" coming up short!! It's all about you today!

DAY 193

Let bygones be bygones! Family is family, friends are hard to come by and foes well, leave them where they are!! Forgive quickly, don't let things build up or linger.

Let bygones be bygones!

DAY 194

In this life, we have to do what works for our individual selves. I know we've all come in contact with people that have used the term, "if I were you!" Guess what? If you were me, you'd do it just the way I did it!!! Why? "Because you're me." Some have to do it cussing and fussing. Some have to do it silently and with their eyes closed, or perhaps some do it by yelling and screaming. I have to do it with God's help. Without it, I have and will make so many (more) mistakes. I'm still talking about life. It will take you fast, and if you're not careful and watchful, you'll get caught up quick!

Find a way to keep your peace, joy, and sanity. Life is short, then you'll die!!

DAY 195

I will admit that I'm "A piece of work." Will you admit the things that you need to work on? A lot of times, we're choosing not to take responsibility for ourselves, nor do you find any wrong within ourselves. It's always her, him, them, or they! Take a look in the mirror and look really good. I promise you there is something that needs tending to. If EVERYONE is saying "you're mean," then guess what? You're Mean!

Stop pointing the finger and look at yourself. You'll be glad you did. Acknowledgment makes for a better you!

DAY 196

*L*ove yourself more and more each day. Do something nice for YOU at least once a month!!

DAY 197

Why do you name him/her a friend? Have you weathered any storms with them? Did they stay through childbirth, divorce, and or your plain ole stupid times? Sometimes we appoint people to the friendship role too fast. We don't even know what their motives or intentions are. We have to be incredibly careful claiming individuals that may very well be denying us.

Wait some things out. You might save yourself a whole lot of unnecessary anger. True friendship is for life!

DAY 198

Is it raining in your life right now, is it sunny, is it gloomy, or is it an all-out blizzard? We go through seasons in this walk. Sometimes it will be the greatest summer you've ever had, then there will be the worst winter you've ever experienced. One thing is for sure, things don't stay the same. Always look for the rainbow after the rain. Trouble doesn't last always. It may seem like the end by looking at the trees, but just wait until the leaves start to form again and the flowers bloom if you hang in there. Before you know it, you'll be smelling the roses!!

Gear up for the weather all over again. Seasons change, and some are better than others. Just dress for the weather.

DAY 199

Have you ever imagined life without limbs, sight, or hearing? Do you know of anyone with any of these disabilities? We often go through our day complaining about how bad we have it, not realizing that someone is way worse off than you! We are so fortunate and won't even acknowledge it. Take a day to just give thanks and not complain.

Use a day to build up and not tear down a day just to compliment and not criticize. Pick a day to Look at life differently. Try it; you just might like it.

DAY 200

Along the way, something got in the way!! Pride, stubbornness, greed, selfishness, vanity, Something!! The outcome was not considered, nor did anyone look down the road to see if it was a dead end. There was no mental flight of the end of the night!! Folks just went along, ignoring every warning sign, yield sign, and stop sign. There will always be daggers and things to come at you along the way.

So, keep looking up so you'll know when to duck and dodge. Things can be avoided if you pay attention!!

DAY 201

Simple words to live by: Don't say you can if you can't. Don't say you do if you don't. Don't say you will if you won't. We make so many promises. Some we keep, some we plan to keep but don't, and some we have no intention of keeping.

If you say it, make good on it. If you can't, then don't say it. Be a person of your word, because once your word is stripped by lies, deceit, and broken promises, That's it!!

DAY 202

*A*re you grateful for life, health, and strength? Do you ever wake up with so much gratitude that you can't think about anything else but being alive? Your mindset is that life is so short, and that person who left the earth last year, last month, last week, or last night even, could've been me, but I'm still here. You begin to say, "Forget the dumb stuff. I'm just happy to be alive!!" Enjoy your days as gifts and live every moment like it's your birthday.

Put on a different party hat every day and change things up ."ENJOY" YOUR DAYS ON TOP OF THE DIRT!!

DAY 203

Some people are most happy when others are at their lowest. I love it when "after being tested," one can regain their composure from "What was meant" to be the hardest blow ever!! Be it finances, tragedy, drug addictions, character assassination, illness, and yes, "Marital Challenges." Life will throw you plenty of curveballs. However, it's up to "US" to stay on the field or take your bat and go home.

Stay in the game and focus on what's important. If it's worth it, position yourself to batter up!

DAY 204

If you have to turn into a spy or private investigator in your relationship, and you can't leave the house for work or a trip without feeling insecure, you're in trouble. If your fear is that he/she is talking to someone else, texting, or inboxing someone, you really need to re-evaluate some things.

If you don't feel safe with whomever you're with, then you're in danger!! Get help.

DAY 205

Wake up before you miss work! ~**John 9:4 I must work the works of him that sent me, while it is day: the night cometh, when no man can work.**~

DAY 206

What makes you the happiest? What puts the biggest grin on your cute face? What thoughts light up your entire day? When you think your day will be a crappy one, think about all the good in your life. Reflect on what has given you the most pleasure, and marinate.

Don't sit and waddle in an angry Pit. It leads to nothing but stress and anguish! Learn how to encourage yourself up out of bad days and make it a great day!! Life is too short!!

DAY 207

At some point, life will come to an end. So, do all you can, say all you can, go as many places as you can, right your wrongs, cross your "T's," dot your "I's," for you know NOT when your end is. At least try it!

Take no prisoners and have no regrets.

DAY 208

If you want to have life, you have to stop hanging out with the dead things of this world! Put away deadly talk that could eventually claim your life. For whatsoever you speak shall be.

Walk as though you already have it, declare life in a dying world! Make every moment count!!!

DAY 209

True Friendship isn't someone in agreement with everything that comes out of your mouth or the approval of your every action. True friendship is not me being afraid to disagree with you when you're completely and clearly in error!

Be thankful for the Friends that God lent you. They are few and far between!

DAY 210

The bible tells us to be content in whatever state we find ourselves in. Although sometimes you may say this is harder than anything I've ever experienced, and you wonder why it is that you were chosen to go down this particular path. You still have to be content in knowing that all things are working for your good.

Although you may feel like you're sinking, grab hold and don't let go. There is a blessing in being content!!

DAY 211

What traits (As a man/woman) do you admire in yourself, and what flaws do you focus so heavily on? Do you walk around with your head held high, or are you looking over at the next man/woman, coveting "ALL" that they possess? First, you have to locate your inner Beauty then work your way to the outside. This may take a moment, yet. While you're working on loving yourself, you don't have time to be envious of another. God made all of us delightful; some may need to take the time on themselves to see it. The amount of time wasted to glare at another can be used to embellish your magnificent self!!

Pssst, don't look over there, LOOK IN THE MIRROR!

DAY 212

What hat will you wear today? Will it be your mommy/daddy hat? Your policeman or military hat? A daughter/son hat? A teacher, preacher, or reacher? A friend or confidant? Whatever the hat, put it on and wear it out! The role to you may seem redundant and not so rewarding, But to the person on the other end of the scope, you're their hero!

Keep doing what you're doing. If it doesn't lend a financial gain…the seed you plant today will come up again. Keep up the great work!!

DAY 213

What is today to you? Is it your birthday, your anniversary, the start of your life? Is it "what you would call it?" THE WORST DAY OF THE YEAR!? God calls it a brand-new mercy! This means that this is a day to right your wrongs, forgive, have compassion, show love, etc. Actually, this day is about freedom! Some may call it a bad day because they're so bound up by the cares of this world. (It should not be!!) All God wants you to do is wake up and give the rest to him!

If you'd cast your burdens on the man that can and will handle it, you'll see, TODAY will turn out to be a phenomenal, awesome, and marvelous Day!!

DAY 214

Good Morning. Beautiful has the sound "Be You" in it!!! Think about that, don't be defined by anyone else's beauty. You don't have to mimic someone else to be beautiful, Just Be You!!!!#DDB INSPIRATION#

DAY 215

Life is about possibilities. It's possible to succeed. It's possible to travel and see the world. It's possible to start over when you think life has failed you. As long as you're breathing, you can possibly Do something great! Don't give up; keep on going. Start over a million times if you have to. Tomorrow is not promised, but if you are awarded a new day at life.

Take it as a chance to keep living. A lot of people plan to take their life. YOU LIVE YOURS!

DAY 216

Let's do something different today and discuss: My pet peeves in a relationship are lying, cheating, and Not spending quality time with the one I'm with... And the list goes on! What is one or some of yours?

DAY 217

What is your testimony? Did you survive a car accident? Were you shielded from a stray bullet? Did you escape an abusive relationship unscathed? Was your marriage mended? Did God save a loved one? Were you unclamped from the hold of drug addiction? Whatever yours is, are you using it as a tool? There are so many lives that can be changed just by hearing the words "He did it for me!" Or " But God!" Someone can make it just because you made it!

When the opportunity arises, SHARE YOUR STORY. Someone's life depends on it!!

DAY 218

Time does more than heal wounds; time allows space to right your wrongs, creates opportunities to grow, and opens up the door to success. If used wisely, so much can be accomplished. If looked upon positively, there's so much that can be done.

Maximize your time. You never know when it will run out!

DAY 219

People will chew you up and spit you out if you're not conscious. Some individuals look for a weakling to pounce on, and if your back is turned, or you're somewhere running your mouth and not paying attention, you will be their next victim! Be aware of your surroundings and watch for those lurking to steal your joy and peace of mind! Stay alert, stay prayerful, and focused!

Don't let the enemy come in and disrupt your cool, calm day. 24 hours isn't long enough to be miserable halfway through it. Claim your WHOLE day!!

DAY 220

Wake up this morning telling yourself that this will be a great day and walk. Accordingly, don't let anyone or anything interfere with the mission ahead. If it rains, pop-out your umbrella and keep it pushing. If it storms... Go inside, muffle the sound, and continue to have your party. You determine the outcome of your day.

Place all of your efforts in the success of your phenomenal day!

DAY 221

Don't let people drive you to jail or to an early grave moral of this inspiration is people will do things that will have you ready to snap or commit suicide, don't do either!! You have to realize which persons to align yourself with and those you absolutely should not! Some are here on earth as a direct assignment to ruin your life, then some are here merely to sharpen your iron.

Make sure you thoroughly sift through the pile of "so-called" rubbish. You don't want to toss the ones that you truly need for your voyage!

DAY 222

Sometimes you have to ask yourself what's more important... Getting it in or MAKING it in!! Some get so caught up in the right now part that they'll miss the everlasting part. These pleasures are temporary, but nothing compares to what's to come.

DAY 223

Do you ever just need the Lord to help you? Do you ever ask him, "Lord, what are you doing?" Where am I? Who are these people? Sometimes you may feel like he's made a mistake, or maybe you made a mistake, and he's just letting you sit there and think for a moment! Maybe he's saying, "My child, this is what happens when you do things on your own!" Or "this is what happens when you venture off without my leading!" Or this just may be the path that he's intended for you to take all along! "The Process leading up to the Promise!" The process hurt, but the promise is ever so rewarding. Whether this was God's plan, or whether he's using YOUR plan as a "Glory tool," it's all working together.

God has a way of taking what almost killed you and turn it around to give you life. You'll understand it better by and by.

DAY 224

Where is your positive talk? We walk around declaring defeat; we pronounce financial death over our lives because of what it looks like right now. We have to begin to speak life to our situations and see tomorrow through the eyes of faith! Tell yourself; it won't always be like this, Trouble don't last always, and God is yet working it out.

As long as you sit in misery, you will never get up and do something!! GET UP!

DAY 225

You don't have to do Tit for Tat because whatever one sows, they will surely reap. Don't waste your time getting back at someone.

Continue to do good, and before you know it, that seed that was planted is coming up.

DAY 226

Some things in life you should just learn from!! If it almost killed you before, why embark upon it again? We are creatures of habit, and we'll experience a thing 99 times until it finally clicks, and you say, "This is not good for me!" Creeping while married, taking those pills, texting, and driving - whatever the risk, the next time could be fatal. Why is it that one never looks at a thing like, "if I continue in this, this could be bad!! (And it will not only just affect me) Take a mental flight on the road you're on right now. Should you do a U-turn immediately, proceed with caution, then pull over, or is it all good in the neighborhood? Accidents aren't just claiming the "one life" nowadays. It's taking all parties involved. So, be careful when you say, "It's just this once!" It may very well be "this once," and the last time you say it!!

Stop, Think, and Flee!

DAY 227

Love is safe, love is pure, love is kind. I don't know how people can mistake love for pain. Love doesn't hurt. Individuals use love to try to hurt, manipulate, and dominate others.

Love is meant to restore and rescue the drowning. When it becomes uncomfortable to be in love, check your relationship before blaming it on the Love.

DAY 228

Don't let your present situation determine your future outcome. It looks bleak, things may be tight, and life may seem hard, but keep your eyes on your destiny and don't allow your circumstances to snuff out the Master's plan!

Stay focused!!

DAY 229

In relationships, distance is not measured in miles but in Love. Two people can be right next to each other yet miles apart, or they can be Miles and Miles apart yet so close in the heart!!!! Sometimes a mate isn't aware that you don't feel their presence because they fail to pay attention to what's right beside them. Yet, the one that is 499 miles away can do those very things that the one right beside you isn't.

Be careful that you are not lonely in a together situation.

DAY 230

Don't shun the advice of everyone. It's worth some investigation. It may save you a great world of hurt, disappointment, and wasted time! Everyone isn't throwing shade; there just may be some validity to some of the warnings. Take Heed!

DAY 231

What's better? Going through and knowing that God will bring you out, or never experiencing anything and not ever knowing what God can do? I'd rather know than to not know. It's always better to have him and not need him than to need him and not have him.

Be reassured today that he'll never leave you nor forsake you. Even when the road is dark, and you can't see your way!

DAY 232

Sometimes we can be wrapped up so much in our own issues that we fail to consider that others may be going through some things as well. We'll cry or fall out because someone doesn't cater to our needs or don't speak to us. We don't know if that person may be on the brink of suicide or have all kinds of things already happening in their lives. Stop assuming just because you're alright, others are alright!

Leave people alone. You don't know what your sarcastic comment will push a person to!!

DAY 233

It's amazing how we as people can go from overjoyed to overwhelmed, or from very sad to ecstatic. Yes, our moods are controlled by the cares and issues of life. We can be smiling one minute, then upon receiving some bad news, we're crying. We could be in a blah or "ugh" state, but if someone puts some money in our hands, that blank stare immediately turns into a sparkly eye. We are up and down, over there, then over here. We are all over the place! A great big roller coaster of emotions. This is just life.

We were created to adjust and readjust. Don't think that you're weird, great news is supposed to alter your day!!!

DAY 234

Don't ever stay in a situation because of people! You could be in an abusive relationship (physically, mentally, or verbally). But because you're worried about what others will say, you'll stay. Or It could be that you won't give something a chance because others are speaking ill of it. So, you let it pass to save face with people. The bottom line, people will be people no matter what your decision is!

Do or don't do because it makes you happy, and never give someone else the power to decide for you. You have to live with the decision.

DAY 235

Love YOU like you love others! Crush on you like you're crushing on him/her right now! A lot of time, we'll be head over heels in love with someone and not even "LIKE" ourselves!

You can't expect someone to love you correctly when you don't even love your own self. YOU love YOU!!! Then you can instruct others on how to love you!!!

DAY 236

Are you singing to the tune of your own song, or are you dancing to the beat of someone else's drum? Whether you use your energy on your own mission or you spend your time enhancing the vision of another. Either way, you go home exhausted, feet hurting, and just want to plop down on a couch at the end of a day. If you're going to be worn out and go all out for someone, make sure that someone is YOU. Most of the time, we invest so much into others that we end up shortchanging ourselves.

It's okay to help someone with their endeavors. Just make sure your ultimate goal is to establish your own!

DAY 237

It's easy to say, "I Do" yet difficult to say, "I Don't!" Once you're in a marriage, you can't just not like him/her anymore and get a divorce. Be sure before you do!

It doesn't cost much to get in it, but it cost a heck of a lot to get out.

DAY 238

Sometimes you've got to show a person better than you can tell them. In a lot of relationships, people are not taken seriously. You can warn someone over and over again that they're hurting you And there is but only so much threatening one can do. Either they'll get it, or they need to "get ta steppin'!"

Life is too short to waste your time on someone that is wasting your time!! Set boundaries and stick to them!!

DAY 239

When someone walks off from you, don't be mad at them. Their part in your story is over. Do you ever notice that sometimes when TV try to bring ppl back from the dead and write them back in the story, it becomes a huge mess?

Put your pencil down. God has the Pen!!

DAY 240

The Pruning process is never easy!! However, it is very much needed. Some of "US" have been walking around with the same layers for years and years, season in and season out. Layers and layers of hurt, envy, anger, grudges, and even some people!! Sometimes we have to get naked of things to be clothed with the right thing! Being stripped of some things may make you sad, but it will definitely help you.

Many people can't heal properly because they're carrying around old stuff that no longer fits them. We may have to do a process of elimination. Shave off the old and get the new.

DAY 241

Do get distracted by what's going on around you. Stay focused and plant your eye on your goal. Learn the art of Standing in the face of adversity. Your haters would enjoy nothing more than to see you and your dreams fall, let them whisper, and Conspire tunnel vision is your best friend right now, don't look to the right or the left. Continue on!!

DAY 242

If you're gonna make it through this life, you are going to have to love yourself!! "Nothing" will make you who you are but God's love and the Love for yourself! A new car, a brand-new house, or elevation to the President of the United States won't do it!!

When you love and are content with yourself, all voids are filled. Take a liking to yourself, and you won't be all over the place.

DAY 243

Don't ever let your happiness be dependent upon something or someone you might lose! Whether you have it or not shouldn't determine whether you live or not. Life is way too short for you to be watching others live while you're dying. Look at it like this; if I have it, Great!! If I don't, EVEN GREATER. This just means that God is sending something tailor-made just for me!

What you lose, you'll get back double. In the meantime, don't fret!

DAY 244

Sometimes you want to shout on the mountain top all that you're going through (I know I do). Sometimes the pain of it all seems so unbearable. You feel that surely no one has ever experienced all of this. If so, how did they make it out? How long did it take? Who was there to help them? No one will testify anymore, which makes the individual feel as though they are all alone in their situation and no one feels their pain!

We "AS SAINTS" have to get back to testimonies. Someone will overcome and benefit greatly just by you saying, "I've Been There!!"

DAY 245

You can close your eyes to the things you don't want to see, but you cannot close your heart to the things you don't want to feel!

DAY 246

In your relationship, you may wonder who the weird one is. Is it me, or is it them? We all weren't raised the same way! Some were reared to respect, and some were not. You may have been taught love and affection, while your partner never even witnessed a hug in their home! Perhaps one may have been drilled to apologize quickly, while the other grew up in a house with a bunch of stubborn mules! You may have been raised to fear the Lord, but he or she doesn't even believe that there is even a God! Some were taught to put their socks on before their pants, while others may say, "What difference does it make?" Am I weird because I do things differently? Whose way is the right way anyway? The argument can go on and on. But if you're going to make it, you must learn to agree to disagree. Your way may sound biblical, but there's only one BIBLE!!!

DAY 247

The purpose of LIFE is to Live it, not Waste it! You are to seize the time, not let it pass you by! We dwell so much on yesterday that we let today slip right through our fingers. Too much time is spent on past failures and mistakes. We need to become more conscious of our surroundings. Things in the world are getting worse and clearly not better!

Focus more on Life itself!

DAY 248

Did you ever tell yourself, "I'm going to spend the rest of my life with Him/Her," and now that person is nothing but a silent memory? You can be head over heels in love with that person, not knowing that it was only for a season. I don't bash someone or think ill of an ex if "WE" didn't make it. I just say, "Every relationship isn't meant to last forever!" Although no one wants to waste valuable and precious time, that's just how the cookie crumbles! Some relationships teach you some things for the next one. Some are here to make you appreciate your upcoming marriage. Sometimes we get too settled in and unpacked…only to realize that this was just a vacation. We try to create eternity out of a temporary situation!

Don't get upset over a short-lived fling. It just may be preparing you for the real thing!

DAY 249

Do you ever use the words, "This is driving me crazy!"?? It/He/She may, in fact, be getting on your last nerve But never give something or someone the power to drive you crazy! You will be locked up in a padded room, waiting for your next dose of antidepressants, while the person who drove you to this state is on to the next.

Keep your mind guarded. Avoid people, places, and things that come to hinder your peace of mind.

DAY 250

If you're not being treated with the love & respect you deserve, check your "PRICE TAG." Perhaps you have marked yourself down. It's "YOU" who tell ppl what you're worth by what you accept.

Get off the "CLEARANCE RACK" and get behind the glass where they keep the "VALUABLES." Bottom line "VALUE" yourself!!

DAY 251

Time truly brings about change. One day you can hit rock bottom, and over time you would have gained "everything" back and then some. One day you could be madly in love with someone, and the next day another individual is sleeping in your bed. One day you could be killing mad at someone, but as time goes on, you would have mended things, and now you guys operate as though there weren't any altercations at all.

Time can be for you or against you. It could help you or hurt you. Use it wisely; you don't have "Forever."

DAY 252

I can't control what life serves me, but I can certainly choose what to chew and what to spit out. What determines my level of intelligence is how I respond or choose not to respond to certain things. Everything doesn't deserve a response, nor does it need to be digested. Life is so short lately that it's almost "HIP" now to be the peacemaker. Isolating myself from the foolery doesn't make me an introvert. It creates more time for growth because the less you're consumed with the unnecessary, it opens you up and allows for the necessary space.

Steer clear of nonsense so you can drive straight into your purpose!

DAY 253

Today is a new day!! A brand-new chance to live, love, and laugh!! Use what hurt you yesterday, use who betrayed you yesterday, and utilize what you didn't achieve yesterday as a steppingstone for today. We have to stop getting stuck in the ruts of the past.

If it's a new day, you have time to change things. Don't dwell; just do it!

DAY 254

*I*f we fill our days with regrets of the downfalls of the past and with anticipation of the struggles of tomorrow, we have no "Today" in which to be thankful.

Embrace that place of peace and contentment and Live Freely!

DAY 255

Life isn't long enough to spend it tearing someone else down. There's an old saying; "shut your mouth, keep your teeth!" You're gonna be old, grey, and toothless. Doing the same things. If you can't build someone up, use your time to work on "YOU!" There's so much to be done in your own yard, you don't have time to be counting the leaves in your neighbor's yard! As a people, we are just nosy creatures, always wanting to know what someone else's plans are. What "they" are doing now, what they wore, who they're involved with, mind your business and worry about you!

Build your empire and leave theirs alone!! End of story!

DAY 256

*A*re you taking a long ride? A nice little journey it feels like you haven't stopped in years? You've been in the valley, over the mountain, through the woods, a nonstop bike ride down a long, steep, and bumpy hill!! You ask yourself, "did I miss a turn?" No, keep going. Because when you reach your destination, you'll be able to help someone else with directions.

You can't be a GPS to places you have no knowledge of! Your trip just might shorten someone else's trip!! Keep going!

DAY 257

Sometimes God doesn't need to make the lightning flash 3 times in a row or the light to flicker 2 times. Some things are just plain as day and right in front of your face!!! You know some things are RIGHT to do, and then there are those things that you know are definitely WRONG, and you shouldn't do them. Be very mindful of positions and places you allow yourselves in. You know what you can handle and what you cannot!!

Don't keep going without being able to find your way back. Always leave your droppings of breadcrumbs, meaning always leave a trail back to God!!

DAY 258

What is your ultimate goal? What action have you put in motion towards that Goal? Are you going to let yet another year drive past you and wink? We don't necessarily need to make New Year's resolutions, but there comes a time when we need to get tired of the same ole' pit!!

Life is short, and I'm sure you want it to be said that (in this lifetime) you've done SOMETHING! Start today!

DAY 259

*D*o you ever ask yourself, why doesn't so-N-so like me? You inquire, what have I ever done to them? The truth is, if you didn't do anything to them 9 times out of 10, it's not you, it's them! We have to learn to love ourselves enough to stop getting stressed out over why she or he doesn't like me. Sometimes people can be so fickle-minded that they will conjure up reasons why they don't like a person… So, focus on YOU liking YOU, and carry on!

You'll find that you can like "yourself" better than that stranger EVER Could!!

DAY 260

If a person hasn't done anything to you personally, don't let what others say about a person make "your" mind up about them. A lot of friendships have been lost over third-party garbage! Sometimes if you get to know a person for yourself, you will find that they are actually and "in fact" pretty cool. Form your OWN opinion!

DAY 261

World's most beautiful words "BUT I LOVE YOU." World's most painful words "I LOVE YOU, BUT..." In school, I learned that what came before the "BUT" is canceled out! So, if one says; But, I love you!! This means that no matter what has taken place, I still love you!! I love you, but Means; There are conditions to this thing I love you, but I'm "in love" with someone else. Or I love you, but love isn't enough!!

Where the "BUT" is placed tells you where you are placed!! Listen to the verbiage!!

DAY 262

Never call your word into question with lies, deceit, or misrepresentation. Create credibility by honoring your word!!

DAY 263

We have no idea what tomorrow brings, but we do know who is doing the carrying! Place your fate in the hands of someone that cares for you and will take care of you!

DAY 264

Food for thought

How do you know He/She is the one?

Do you truly love them, or is it lust?

Do they add to or subtract from your life?

Are you better with them, or could you do bad all by yourself?

Can your family and friends see the difference this person has made since your meeting them?

Do you imagine life with or without them? (there's a difference)

Do you still get chills up and down your spine when you're in their presence?

Questions only you can answer... Something to think about.

DAY 265

There are so many ways to be happy, i.e., Go to the movies, eat your favorite food, spend your paycheck on something you really want, Meet someone new, etc.

There's only one way not to be happy choose not to! You can do more with happiness than you can being unhappy.

DAY 266

Do you ever comb through your life to see what it is that you can improve on? Do you reflect and say, "Hey, I was doing this exact same thing this time last year!" Sometimes we'd like to blame people, places, and things for our stagnation. But the truth is, if we would've just done some things differently or had taken an alternate route, perhaps we'd be further along than we are today. Don't give people that much power that if it weren't for her, I wouldn't be going through this, or he's the reason I'm in this predicament!! No, your life is YOUR life, and if "YOU" don't get a hold of it, you will be mirroring this year the same next year! Get a grip on your own life!

Stop blaming others if you're choosing not to do some new things. Your results stem from YOUR decisions!

DAY 267

It's a brand-new day, and you should be happy to be alive! I mean, sure, there is something to complain about, but one thing you can't deny is that God woke you up just in time to live! You have the opportunity to do all the things you did not complete yesterday. You can forgive, you can ask for forgiveness, you can do a kind deed, most of all, you can LOVE!!

You are afforded another chance to create a greater you; accept this new mercy and use it wisely. You don't know what tomorrow holds.

DAY 268

Are you aware that your whole life can be altered in a matter of minutes? One wrong move, one selfish act, a car accident, or that unexpected news from your health care provider. Today could be great, but tomorrow could be full of streaming tears. You could be in the White House today but living under a bridge tomorrow. Married today and on your way to a divorce lawyer tomorrow. Sure, we have long term goals, but you never know what life will be like in the next five years. We need to appreciate the people around us and celebrate every birthday "as if" it was our last. Time waits for no one, and tragedy chooses whom he pleases.

Go back inside and tell them you love them, call Cousin Lu Lu up and fix things and resolve those issues before going to bed!! #ShouldaCouldaWoulda!

DAY 269

If you were told that this was your very last Sunday of life, what would you be doing right now? How would you be preparing? What would be the very first thing that you would do upon waking this morning? Would you be picking out the best outfit to go give God your Best, last praise, or would you be running around like a chicken with your head cut off trying to get your incomplete affairs in order? Something to think about, huh?? Ima just leave it right here for us to ponder.

DAY 270

If someone would have described your life as it is today to you years ago, would you have been racing to get here, or would you have killed yourself to avoid this catastrophe? The reason we are not let in on the story of our lives is that we'll move out of turn; either we'll rush things, or we'll abort our destiny. Everything we encounter is needed for the conclusion. We don't get to choose to edit some parts. The Good, the bad, and all of the middle make for an outstanding you! Like me, I know you'd prefer that some people, places, or things be eliminated but how could there be beautiful flowers with no rain.

We need all seasons of life to create balance. Embrace what is, so you can appreciate what's to come.

DAY 271

Do you ever think you want something so bad, but for some reason, God won't release it to you? You cry, pray and throw a fit. But you still don't get it! Or have you ever specifically asked God for something, but he gives you the total opposite? Why is this? What is this? Who is this? "You ask." You told me to make my request known, Lord!! I was specific in my request. Do we not know that God knows what's best for us, and what looks good to "US" may not always be the best thang for us! Sometimes the devil sends "desirable things" to destroy us. But the things God sends will make for a prosperous life!!

We have to learn to desperately accept what God allows and go with his plan Because, in the end, it'll all work together!

DAY 272

Always maintain a level of respect for yourself! No matter what someone else says or does, you monitor You! Never unclothe your entire being. Have them walk away wondering, "did what I say affect him/her?" You don't have to give a reaction to every act committed against you. Learn the art of restraint.

Save your anger for the important situations.

DAY 273

Imagine if the world was filled with people just like you! If everyone acted like you, dressed like you, sang like you, took care of their affairs just like you, how would the world be? Something to think about!!

DAY 274

What you have bottled up can kill you! It causes stress that leads to death, anger that could lead to death, depression that could potentially be deadly. You feel like you sound like a broken record to your family, so you hold it in. If you tell the wrong person, your business will be everywhere. So again, you just hold it in. I say friends are not your friends if you can't release to them.

Don't keep things shut up inside. It's safer to explode on the outside of you than on the inside of you.

DAY 275

*L*ife is filled with so many unstable relationships. You're with this one today and tomorrow "this is REALLY the one!" Either you love them, or you don't. "Not" I did, but now I don't!! We as a society have too many options. We trade in EVERYTHING for a newer model. When this gets too old, I'll get a younger one. Why not invest in what's carried you all of these years?! I'm just saying!!

DAY 276

Determine your "own" worth instead of letting Someone else tell you what you're worth. Most of the time, we are worth way more than how people treat us, talk to us, and how much time people give us! We have to stop allowing people to give us Vienna sausages when we deserve steak! Don't sit in your chair wondering why he chose her over you. You tell yourself there must be someone way better for me! If that interview didn't go well and that man didn't hire, you tell yourself it's their loss, and there must be something tremendously greater!

Don't let someone else's decision be your destiny. YOU have the last word!

DAY 277

Do you know any religious Devils? One's that are religious in one conversation and the devil in another? One that is quoting scriptures on Facebook in the morning, then by night cussing someone out on Facebook! One that loves you with the love of the Lord today and is running you down in a few days. I'm confused. I mean, no one is perfect, and I'm certainly not judging. But you can't be a son or daughter of someone and not display some of their attributes. If you're going to be a Christian, Be Christ-like.

If you're going to be devilish, then stop professing to know Jesus! To know him is to love him, and to love him is to keep his commandments!!

DAY 278

Sometimes you just need peace and quiet to think, gather your thoughts and get your mind right. When you're around people on their cell phones, people listening to their music loudly, children calling your name. Sometimes you have to steal away to be able to have some quiet and alone time with God. Too much going on at once is distracting, and if you're not careful, alert, and aware. You'll start to listen to all those things the devil is telling you! Oh Yes, Satan has devices, and he's ready to catch you off guard, so you will get off course! You should take any opportunity to refresh, regroup and refocus. There are so many hurts and disappointments that we can sit and remind ourselves of. But a mind cluttered with God diminishes the debris of the enemy. Go to the Park, sit in a closet, or find a place where you can release it all to God so he can receive it and redirect you!

The best person to tell your problems to is the one that can "ACTUALLY" do something about it.

DAY 279

Whenever you're going through tribulations in your life, and you're wondering, "Where is God?" Just remember the teacher is ALWAYS silent during test-taking time. Hang in there. I know you may feel like you're going through it alone. But "Trust Me," He is right there! Test and trials come to make you strong and knowledgeable. If God jumped in every time and shielded you from every hurt, disappointment, and more, you wouldn't know or have experienced anything. Sometimes another person's hope is in knowing that you made it through the storm and the rain. We are the mouthpieces of God telling a hopeless world that there is a way out. But you've got to go through!

You're taking away someone's lifeline when "you" give up midstream and your end was just around the corner. Pass your test so you can help someone study for theirs.

DAY 280

Why worry about insignificant people? If they don't matter, then what they say matters less!! Never let the comments of "a nobody" determine the outcome of your day. Ignore a gnat, and it will bug someone else.

Don't be moved, don't swat at it, don't even tell someone else that it's flying around. Just simply continue on as if it's not there!! Leave worry up to worried folks!!

DAY 281

*L*adies:

Do you love yourself? All through life, "We've" waited around for that "one" to come into our lives and love us! We're looking all around. In restaurants, bars, grocery stores, on the Internet, and even churches, but the question is, DO YOU EVEN LOVE YOURSELF? YOU have to 1st love yourself to know what true love is. A lot of times, we don't even know what we're worth because we just don't love ourselves. If you tap into the "YOU" that God created, whether he shows up this year or never...you'd be content. That "one" should be an add-on, not the total you. Because you should be you whether they are on the scene or not. When you find yourself, you'll be less angry, less grumpy, and the people around you will be better off. Don't contemplate, be content; don't worry, just wait; don't bark, just bask in loving yourself... and just when you're not looking, someone is lurking and admiring that "you" that has been cultivated just by the glow of "YOU LOVING YOU!"

DAY 282

Be careful about looking over into someone else's lawn. The grass may appear to be greener, but you have no idea what you're seeking after you've lived in that house. My grandmother always says, "You know whatcha got, but you don't know whatcha might get!" You'd better stay where you are!! Don't go from someone loving you into the arms of someone "only" lusting after you. Don't leave a provider for a loser. Don't leave a good father for someone that only wants you and NOT your children. Don't leave one that spends all his time with you for one that you'll never even know where he is. Don't leave one that would care for you on your sickbed for one that will quickly put yo' tail in a nursing home.

Don't make your bed hard, fluff your pillows, clean up your house, fertilize your own grass!! Stay out of that window wishing!

DAY 283

Giving all your problems to God allows him to show your enemies who he is You don't have to brag or boast, just silently whisper to God; (will you please handle this?) He can avenge you far better than you could ever imagine!

Turn it over to him. He can work it out!!#DDB INSPIRATION#

DAY 284

What is love? Something that consumes your whole being. Who is love? Someone that monopolizes your entire life. Your world!! Where is love? In the pit of your stomach, in your head (your thoughts, dreams, etc.), in your conversation, in your actions! When is love? Every second, minute, and hour of the day, all month and yearlong! How is love? Breathtaking, overwhelming, phenomenal, a breath of fresh air, a risk worth taking!!! Love!!!

One "MUST" experience it at least once. There's nothing like it.

DAY 285

*L*ove on purpose!! Sometimes it takes you by surprise. It creeps up on you before you even know it, and you can't always tell your heart who to love; it just happens! However, those that are not so lovable grab your instructions (the Bible) and go to work on them! It's easy to love those who love you back.

Try it on those who "you know" would stab you in the back the first chance they get! Practice loving instead of leaving.

DAY 286

What does today mean to you? Is it just a normal day of school or work? Is it a day full of errands? Is it the date of birth of a loved one? Is it a day to complain because it's yet another Monday? (Uugghh) We rarely or ever look at today as a day to start over Another chance to take my life to a whole new dimension. If allotted, "New days" are given as a fresh start. We just have to embrace them for what they are intended for, not just a normal calendar day routine.

Wake up today, not just for heading to work, school or errands. Clothe yourselves with the mindset that I'm headed to my destiny, the most fabulous outfit anyone can wear!

DAY 287

*L*ove like no one is watching!! I love to see people interact with care and concern like no one else is in the room but the two. What if there were no social media to brag on your love? What if there were no text messages to apologize through, no roses to do all the work, no money to buy an "I'm sorry" or everything else we use to speak for us. Could you express your love? I'm saying that sitting in a cold, dark cave with no witness, love should still be easy. A stranger should be able to look at two people in love and say, "I want that!" If you don't share that with the one you're with, maybe you need to eliminate all the outside forces and go back to the basics. Love is pure. It doesn't need all of that stuff that contaminates it!

DAY 288

Who are you when "everything" about you is a lie? Your address is a lie, your name is a lie, where you work is a lie (Tommy), how much you make is a lie, and who your friends are is a lie! What you think of yourself is a lie! What "Allow," people say about you is a lie!! Life must be miserable telling one lie to cover up another and telling an even bigger one to conceal all of them. A day of all of that surely must be exhausting! If you can't be yourself around people, then either you're living wrong "or" those people aren't your friends. Life is too short to not live it honestly and fully! What are you afraid of? Who has scared you out of your true identity? Be free to be you, even if you lose people. If people don't like you when you're yourself, Dump 'em'!!! "ONLY YOU" can be the best YOU there is!! Practice it!! Life will be so much LESS stressful.

"TRY THIS"

Hi, my name is ___! And your opinion of me doesn't matter!!

DAY 289

Some changes look negative on the surface, and you really don't like change. But you will soon realize that space is being created in your life for something new to emerge. Things have been the same for so many years and on so many levels yet, with no productivity. It's time for something new, a direction of progression.

Do things differently and get better results!

DAY 290

Although we make "What we feel are" the worst mistakes of our lives, it's all in the plan!! What doesn't kill you will definitely strengthen you.

DAY 291

You ever met the most trifling someone. Their life goal was but to take you down? They'll spy on you and place themselves where you are just to find something on you to discredit your character! They're miserable, and their main mission on earth is to add some company to their misery. How do you avoid these creatures? I say you continue to live right and put God on them. This fight is way too big for you. These people have low self-esteem, and they'll stop at nothing to drag you down with them.

Don't defend yourself; the battle is not yours. This is a job for SuperGod!

DAY 292

What is your trust in? People, places, or things? We'll trust a certain someone because they've never let us down, we'll move to a certain place because it seems to be less crime, and we'll just flop down on a couch because we trust that it will hold us "Truth is" You never know with people. They are different ways on different days, and you can't be too sure about places because there is crime now, in places where there has never been before. You never know about things because they don't make furniture like they used to. Put no trust in man, places, or things!!

Trust the God of your salvation. He truly has your best interest at heart!!

DAY 293

"Love," if Genuine, is so amazing! Not this lip action that people are engaging in nowadays. When one loves another, it shows up in their behavior. Love is not ONLY talked, but also seen through the eyes and felt through the touch. Although "I love You" is great to hear, it's even better when experienced. I don't know that I believe in fairy tales, but I do know that there is such a thing as loving someone beyond words. Beyond uttering those three words, there is great demonstration. When you love someone, that person is on your mind, it shows in your demeanor, and protrudes through in your attitude! And even though you may not always agree with the one you love, there will still be no question.

Get you some love today and see won't it revamp your whole life.

DAY 294

*E*ither love them or leave them! Show them the love they deserve or leave and let their true love do their thing. A lot of people are just occupants of space. They are not doing what they came to do! Humans are meant to love and be loved. But sadly enough, some aliens were thrown in the bunch. When it's hard for a person to love, I question their DNA because God (our father) created us in his image.

If you're in something questionable, step back and talk about things because "NOTHING" can be done without Love!!

DAY 295

IF YOUR PRESENCE DOESN'T ADD VALUE 2 MY LIFE, YOUR ABSENCE WON'T BE WORTH ONE RED CENT$!!!!! Stop letting people be the worth of your existence. I'm me because of who I am, not because you're around! With or without you, I'm still that chick. So whether you're present, absent, or tardy, the show will still air. Before I let someone be the missing piece, I'll throw the whole puzzle away.

Never give one that much power that if they leave, you'll die. You put on your grown man/woman outfit and Live EVEN BETTER!

DAY 296

When a person has been practicing something for a long time, i.e., smoking, cheating, bad attitude, running from relationships; unless they allow God to do surgery on them, it will take a great deal to stop. There has to be a brand-new way of thinking. The desire to change has to be greater than the desire to continue. People can tell you all day that you are in error, but you will somehow wind up right back there until you see the wrong in it. Change is about Choice, life is about living and learning, and maturity is about growing from past mistakes..

Different results come about by different approaches. If you've been doing it this way "All of your life," try taking another approach!

DAY 297

Do you feel like you're the only one loving? You're the only one sacrificing? You're the only one keeping the peace? Does it seem as though you are putting in more than you're receiving? And what you're giving out isn't being reciprocated? Are you really serious about being a good person, while others are nonchalant and will provoke an episode every chance they get? What do you do? Do you just say, "forget it," and give them a dose of "the erupted volcano?" I say continue to operate in self-control. God will not see his child in pain long!

Stay true to the vow you made to change and leave the whooping up to the one that's got you covered! You're too cute to fight. The battle isn't yours anyway!

DAY 298

Want to know what's in your heart?!? Listen to what comes out of your mouth!! I often hear people say, "I'm not bitter, or I'm not jealous, and I'm not mad!" But what you're saying doesn't match what you're saying. You say you love them, but circumstances say differently. Get a person drunk or angry, and you'll know exactly what's in their heart.

Don't do what they want you to do and watch what they do! Guard your heart; your mouth will tell on you!

DAY 299

No matter where you go or how grown you become, you still ought to be accountable to someone! It may be a spouse, your parent, your Pastor, or even your child. Nowadays, there is too much going on for at least one person not to know your whereabouts. You could be slumped over somewhere etc. etc. Police brutality, street violence, and just plain olé heart failure has really claimed the lives of our people.

top worrying about who's in your business! You don't want to be yelling for help, and no one knows where the yelling is coming from.

DAY 300

Never walk around looking down on others. Today you could be on the mountain top, and tomorrow you could be at the bottom. You are where you are because of God. But don't get to acting like you're on his level. You didn't part the Red Sea, you don't perform miracles, you can't raise the dead. And You're certainly not responsible for anyone's health or wealth! Be who you are, and that's it! Don't rub your stardom in other folk's face because you're no better than I, and I'm no better than you. We are all God's children!

Be a good steward over what you have. It could be here today and gone Just like that!!!

DAY 301

*E*verything around you will serve different purposes. The chair is to sit on, the bed is to sleep on, the table is to eat on, the floor is to walk on, the television is to be watched, and doors are to let you in and out. The same goes for the people that surround you. Some will love you, some will leave you, some will tear you down, then some will build you up. Some will like you, some will not. Some will stay by your side through everything, and some will run at the first chance they get. You have to know that some will reach for your hand and pull you up, while others may be your "footstool" to get up.

Embrace the ones that are here to stay and open the door for the ones that are to leave. But learn each and every lesson from both!!

DAY 302

As humans, we would prefer to live our lives like robots ~vs. ~ letting life run its course. We want to push the green button to get rich, then the yellow button to find the right mate, the green button to get where we're going without delay, the blue button to x people out of our lives, etc. We don't want to suffer any hardships, disagree with our mates or have trouble out of our children. But without any downs, we wouldn't know how to appreciate the ups!! Yes, goes with no, good goes with bad, and so forth and so on. With the pretty magic buttons, our lives would have no balance. I'm me because of all that I've endured, but I'm his (God's) because of his bringing me out.

Let life coast. At the end of the journey, you'll appreciate the trip.

DAY 303

Do you have a song on your heart? Did you know that music soothes? When you're going through tough things, find you a song and quietly hum or softly sing it. Not only will it ease your mind, but it will help you release as well. Instead of sitting and having a pity party, thinking yourself into a suicidal state, or wrestling with yourself about your next move, relax and sing a song. Life is already short, and times are already hard, so we definitely have to find creative outlets.

Don't sit and sulk; move about and sing. It works for me and I'm sure it will work for you!! #SingYourselfHappy

DAY 304

*D*o you ever look in the mirror and admire what you see? That person is beautiful/Handsome. You have to pat your own self on the back, don't let others define you. Look at yourself, and say, Girl/Boy, you are spicy!! At least one day out of the week, get up, wash the crust out of your eyes, put on something cute, and prance around in the mirror. A lot of low self-esteem issues stem from not appreciating the "you" that God created! Don't depend on the compliments of others.

Tell yourself that you've got it going on, and when someone else tells you, it would just confirm what you already know! Love and appreciate your created self!!

DAY 305

Life is full of so many "I love you's, I got you's, I'm in your corners, you know you my dawgs, I'm your ride or dies, and way too many You can trust me(s)!" You just have to rummage through the junk and find what is for you!! Never take something home that will kill you while you're sleeping! A dog (Dawg) will lick you in the mouth, then turn around and bite the hand that feeds it.

Be aware of strays that are walking around with Rabies!

DAY 306

*D*id you not know that your life was mapped out before you entered the world? Every mistake, every trial, every child (miscarriages and abortions included), Marriage #1, 2, 3 & 4! Even though God knew that we'd succumb to our flesh, His plans are "STILL" for us to have life more abundantly, to prosper, and be in good health. His desire is that none of us perish. But it's sad to say that some will still continue in the ways of contradiction. You plan your weekends (without God). We plan our vacations (Without God). We get up some mornings and never even acknowledge God. But he always has us in mind, making plans for us, creating ways to bless us, and protecting us when we didn't even know we were in danger. Life is but a vapor So, close your eyes, trust God, and enter through the gate.

Don't let your steamy hot flesh have you left behind. If you're breathing right now, it's not too late.

DAY 307

Is life hard? Or do I not have on my proper gear? A lot of times, we lose a battle because we weren't prepared. Yes. I know that sometimes we can be caught off guard. But I was once told, "If you stay ready, you don't have to get ready!" We have to stay guarded at all times. Put on the whole armor!! Don't take a stick to a gunfight!! You have to know what you're dealing with and dress accordingly. Life is full of tricks and games, so you have to bring the mind that; I won't be a part of any foolishness today. There's so much gossip and slander. You must pack your mental tape and earplugs. So, you won't participate or entertain any stupid conversations.

The enemy will try his best to draw you into his web, but you have to be alert and ready!

DAY 308

When you've shared with someone all of your life's experiences, hurts, heartaches, pains, disappointments, and things that you've endured, and they turn around and dig the knife deeper, it makes you question their sanity! Are they crazy? Didn't I explain to them that I was cheated on? Don't they know that I've been stabbed in the back many times before this? Didn't I confess to them that Jonny-Ray just up and walked out on me? What's wrong with some people? It almost makes you not want to develop any other new relationships. But then look at all the other great people in the world. Not all humans are insensitive and or heartless! You just have to be extremely careful with whom you sign your heart over.

You can't control what people do to and with you, but you can certainly control how long you will put up with and endure the pain. The timer has beeped on some of this stuff and definitely some of these people!!

DAY 309

Don't be reckless with other people's hearts, and don't put up with people who are reckless with yours. There's a danger in toying with someone's belonging!

DAY 310

When you learn who is with you and who isn't, it is easier to accept some things. When you go in with your eyes wide open, it's almost impossible to fall and get hurt. When people show you who they are and what they're about. Proceed accordingly. Know this Everyone will not ride with you. And that's perfectly fine...just roll with the ones that have and will until the wheels fall off! Don't get yourself all worked up when people aren't there. Too many people in your life isn't a good idea anyway. The More people, the more foolishness you have to contend with.

Don't waste your time on those that are not in your life. Spend your time loving the ones that are!!

DAY 311

Have you been waiting on life to bring about a change? Are you wondering when your day of reaping is? You witness everyone around you being blessed with spouses, jobs, cars, homes, elevation, and even big money!! You ask yourself, "What are they doing that I'm not?" Perhaps "wondering" is ALL you're doing! We have to put a little action behind our faith. Whether it be cleaning up your credit, putting in applications, going to the dealership, or falling on your knees and crying out to God! Asking on Facebook "who's hiring" is not the most productive way to look for a job, and "most great things" don't just knock on your front door. Sometimes, you have to align yourself with your blessing. Ruth positioned herself for Boaz to notice her. Put some lipstick and earrings on, go to the house of God, and "be found" working!

If what you've been doing isn't working, take a different approach. So, you won't be asking the same questions this time next year.

DAY 312

Why do some look to others for affirmation? Why are some people, approval addicts? Who is that important that they are walking around signing off on acceptance letters? You need to declare to yourself that you are just as significant as the people next door, even if they have a Bentley in the driveway. Tell yourself that you are not inferior to anyone. I'm great! Not just because I say so but because God says so! Don't let anyone be the dictator of your life; you create avenues and stimulate your own drive. There is nothing more unattractive than someone that is controlling others. Stand up. You will find that you're of equal statue or maybe even a great deal taller. Usually, people that feel the need to control other's lives are deeply insecure within. They're either trying to prevent others from getting up and walking or rising up to soar. Push their foot off your neck and take your rightful place on "your Own" two feet!!

You're not substandard to anyone. You have your very own purpose; put it in gear and take flight!

DAY 313

*D*on't let life as it is today change your path. Keep your focus; it won't always be like this! Sometimes we give up and turn around a little too soon. If we would have just hung in there for just a little while longer, our change would've come. We have to learn tenacity and patience!! We want a perfect life, but to appreciate a blessing, he (God) had to have blessed you up out of something.

Don't let circumstances deter you, don't let problems delay you, and don't let mistakes keep you from "Your day!" Soon and very soon, if you'd just hold on!!

DAY 314

Don't allow someone that doesn't know you make you get so out of character that you don't even recognize yourself!! You don't want to become someone that they've told people that you were all along. Their job as the devil's Imps is to provoke you. Don't do it, Miss Celie!! Keep your character intact and your reputation free of "Truth" talk. People will lie and spread rumors all day, but don't "you" give them something to discuss. Learn some restraint!! Every little thing isn't worth a response!

Adapt the art of preserving your energy for important things only. Disregard the petty things!!

DAY 315

Relationships are 100/100, not 50/50. Individuals have to give their absolute all to make it work. Don't measure your giving by the others, and don't measure their giving by yours. They may be loving how they were taught to love. Some men and women really don't know that there is a difference between "I love you" and being "in love!" Some men were not raised or taught to love a woman. Their mother failed to think ahead and groom them for adult manhood (as a husband and father). So as his woman, you NOW have to have the wherewithal to teach him how to love "YOU" and all that comes with it. It's a task, but it's doable!

Relationships take patience, but with both parties participating, y'all should be fine. No, it won't always be perfect, but with genuine efforts, it'll be a bed of roses (just remember, though). Roses have thorns!!

DAY 316

It amazes me the advice that people give one another. Didn't you spend 99 years with that man that you're STILL with that had not 1, but 2 babies on you, and your advice to her after only 6 months of marriage is "Child, leave his no-good self!! And you've been putting up with the same drama for 15 years on that job that you're STILL at and advising someone to leave it. And criticizing someone about buying an SUV when gas is so high. Meanwhile, you're catching a ride "with them" because you don't even own a bicycle. People STOP IT!! Stop saying If I "WERE YOU!" The truth is you would do just what I'm doing. Why? Because you "ARE ME!!"

Be what a person needs, stand by them, or get out of their way! And if you don't have sound advice...Hush and JUST PRAY!!

DAY 317

Three things "I HATE" the most and SO VERY PASSIONATELY are: 1. Cheating 2. Gossip & 3. Lying Cheating ruins relationships, Gossip tarnishes Characters, and Lying taints reputations. These 3 are bold and outright killers; there is nothing silent or discreet about them! Beware of a person practicing any of these behaviors.

Life is too short to wake up wearing orange attire every day!

DAY 318

There's only one thing worse than a Cheater; a Cheater with "No Respect!" One that will sit up in the same house and text another man/woman while your significant other is at home; a low-down individual that will bring another man or woman to the same house that they share with their significant other; or that trifling "son of a shoemaker" that will transport another man or woman in the car that is in your name!! Cheating is a horrible thing but cheating with no respect is the absolute worst! I've never and probably never will understand the logic behind having a mate and 4 or 5 others.

Just be single and "free" to mingle with any and everything! Stop ruining lives!!!

DAY 319

True respect for another comes from self-respect. True love for another comes from the love of one's self. True forgiveness for another comes from forgiveness of one's self. True happiness for another stems from the happiness within one's own self. You cannot be to someone else what you're not to yourself. If you're angry, you'll bleed anger; if you're bitter, bitterness is what you'll display. Hurt people hurt people! You can pretend and smile all day but, in your heart, it is what it is.

Get yourself together so you won't have to put up this continued facade!

DAY 320

*D*on't be afraid of new things; just make sure they are biblical. It's a brand-new year. Change is good, doing things new is good; A new job is great, just make sure you leave the old one right. A new home or car is wonderful; just make sure it is financially feasible. A new relationship is awesome; just make sure you close one book before opening another and "PLEASE" make sure he/she isn't someone else's spouse. Sometimes a "New way" is just what is needed!! My Lifestyle, his eating habits, and your way of thinking. And no man puts new wine into old bottles: else the new wine does burst the bottles, and the wine is spilled, and the bottles will be marred: but new wine must be put into new bottles. Mark 2:22.

It's a new year, don't take the old into the new!!

DAY 321

If you think my hands are full, you should see my mind! If you think that's a mess, then take a look at my heart! Many people admire whatever is on the outside but have no idea what's on the inside. Show me a woman with a lot of glitz and glamour. I'll show you a girl that has seen lots of pain and tears.

Don't crave the glory if you don't know her story. Don't begrudge the reign if you've not witnessed her pain!

DAY 322

Life's too short to spend it worrying about people who don't value your relationship. Hold close to those who would panic if they had lost contact with you! Often, what you are to people is a quota met of how many people they can have around them. To have celebrity status or just another number, they need to make "7000 followers" on social media. What you've brought into the new year determines what you will take in the "New Year."

I hope you've packed light. Too much baggage will cost you!

DAY 323

How much joy and contentment are you experiencing in your life right now? It could be one thing in particular that gives you to feel at ease in life. Take it! However, no "ONE" thing should completely take your smile. You should be happier in life now than you've ever been. If you're not, find out what it is that has you bound and release it. We have to create our place of peace. There is no one, no place or thing that should be the driving force behind your continued unhappiness. And if that be the case, then something is definitely wrong. Some people live to take away your giggle, and some things are designed to get you off course, but you have to learn to take a lickin' and keep on tickin'! Don't let one blow knock you out. Situations will certainly arise, but we have to learn to fix what we can and the rest...Turn it over to the one that can. All the while still smiling.

Let life take care of itself. You just live as though your next breath isn't promised because honestly, it isn't!!

DAY 324

The pessimist sees the glass half empty. The optimist sees the glass half full. The realist just sees "a drink" in the glass. And the Extremist (such as I) envisions something else in the glass. We have to learn to see the glass as God sees it. If the Glass is still there, stand still and Wait on the rest… A lot of times, we miss the overflow because we move the glass, trying to fill it up or pour it out.!!

Keep the glass in position and let God control the stream.

DAY 325

How do some of us become so bitter?? Yes, there are tragic things that have occurred in our lives. But are they to such a degree that we are willing to die and go to hell over them? People get angry when they hear the 1st letter of someone's name or the faint scent of someone's cologne. I refuse to let anything or anyone, single or minute thing be the cause of my demise. I mean, it's issue-matic enough going through everyday life And then to leave this earth and go to hell? I DON'T THINK SO!! Sometimes we may need to alter some things in our lives just so we can go to heaven.

Life is too short. Live happy and be free!! Let obstacles make you BETTER, NOT BITTER!!! LET IT GO OR LET THEM GO!! It's not worth it!!! #DDB INSPIRATION#

DAY 326

It's hard at first, but all pain eases after a while. Don't keep putting yourself in positions to keep hurting. Pain is pain. But if you remove yourself, eventually, the pain will stop. Some situations will kill you if you continue in them. No "thing" is worth your life.

Learn the lesson, then move along.

DAY 327

It's not the guns that kill people. It's the Careless person with the gun that kills people. Social Media doesn't destroy Relationships. It's the Care-Less people with the login and password that destroy relationships. We Are The Ammunition!!! We have to learn to stop blaming other sources for our actions. Put that blame where it belongs; if you cheated because you're tired, say that! Don't use the excuse that she let herself go. If you've gained weight from eating too much, admit that! Don't blame it on your thyroid. If you just don't want to live right, confess that!

Don't say the Deacon ran me off!! Stop putting the responsibility of your Care-Less actions elsewhere!

DAY 328

Why are we moved when a person is being themselves? Liars lie, cheaters cheat, and thieves steal! And chances are, if they'll do one, they'll do all three. My mother would say, "If you'd lie, you'd cheat, and if you'd cheat, you'd steal." Also, don't think you have "A Friend" in one of these people. If they lie with you, they'll lie on you. If they cheat with you, they'll sho 'nuff cheat on you, and certainly, if they steal with you, you'd better believe they'll steal from you! Please don't be deceived. You'll end up with your feelings hurt, your name in the mud, and your things missing.

DAY 329

Remove yourself from identity snatchers - people assigned to convince you that you are NOT who God called you to be. Be aware of individuals who do nothing but bring up your past and remind you of what you used to be. Gather your credentials, hold your head up high and yank away from the thief that comes to rob you of who you were born to be! Your name is VICTORY, your name is SUCCESSFUL, your name is BEAUTIFUL!!

You are not who man says that you are. Rather, you are created in the image of Christ. Which makes you Someone Special!!

DAY 330

When someone makes the statement ."You're with my ex" Smile and Say yes, leftovers are actually pretty awesome when properly reheated by someone who knows what they're doing. lol

DAY 331

You ever feel so uncomfortable with your present situation that you could not stop crying? You've ever just questioned and questioned God how and why things are as they are? You ever said to yourself, "I must have jumped out of his will somewhere along my journey because surely this can't be the will of the Lord for my life!" You begin to analyze your time here on earth. You comb through every one of your actions. Lord, was I extremely mean to someone, and now I'm getting it all back? Did I cheat on someone in the past, and what goes around has now come around? Did I forget to pay my tithes, and now I'm cursed with a humongous curse? Lord, every part of me hurts, and if you don't help me soon, I just don't know. I assure you that God feels your every pain, hears your every cry, and knows your every need. Although you may feel alone, He's right there!

When you're at your weakest, that's when you're the strongest because the greater "HE" is "IN YOU!"

DAY 332

If "WE" as a people would just think before we act, there would be a lot fewer divorces, fewer children born out of wedlock, the jails would be a lot less empty. Our churches would be of an even greater capacity. Some of us are so selfish. We do things based on what pleases our own selves at that very moment; things are not thought all the way through. We don't consider the end result of this thing or that thing. We're just enjoying "The Now!"

We all need a chair and a thinking cap. I tell you, life would be so much better!!

DAY 333

*J*ust because someone is running off at their mouth, there's not always a great need to confront them. It's a comedy show!!! It's rude to talk while an individual is on stage!!!

Just crack up, let 'em be a sideshow all by themselves.

DAY 334

Your name may not be "Wonder Woman!" You may not wear the nice gold bracelets that will stop people from doing things. You may not have the long, fancy belt to coerce people into telling the truth. But with God, you do possess a certain power that will certainly make people "Wonder" how you were able to do certain things!

DAY 335

In "MOST" cases nowadays, when you see a man opening a car door for a woman, it can only mean 1 of 2 things. Either the car is new, or the Girlfriend/Wife is.

Ladies, I say whether it's a hooptie or you've been with him 99 years, continue to require to be treated like a queen.

DAY 336

Sometimes we need to look at our situations in a greater light. (And this one is for "Me" as well as you) Holding your peace through turmoil teaches restraint, shows your maturity, and allows God to work. Sometimes that loved one may not get an early release from prison, but the time spent gives them a moment to think, makes them a better individual and allowed God time to work. Some relationships may never be mended. But it kept you on your knees, developed your relationship with God, and it allowed time for Him to work!! All things work together for the Good of them.

Sometimes we're looking for "the Good" to be one thing, but "God" has something totally different and greater in mind! Our way of thinking is not his way of doing!

DAY 337

At what age are we considered grown? What magnitude of the mindset are we considered mature? How much wisdom should be instilled where we're considered wise? How long does it take us to put away childish things once we're no longer a child? In this day in time, we have so many who are no longer in middle/high school but continue to operate as though they are fresh out of elementary school. What grown 35yr old gets joy out of seeing mess get started? What 50-year-old finds pleasure in starting the mess? What 65-year-old you know isn't developed enough in the mind to stop foolishness and steer clear of it?

At some point, the nonsense should aggravate you as much as sin stinks in the nostrils of God! Grow up and outgrow the foolery!

DAY 338

There will come a time when you'll have to stop defending yourself and let God start avenging yourself! You'll find that people that have never even met you before will put a label on you. How do you defend that? They will say you're this and say you're that and cause others to even scratch their heads concerning you. You just have to turn that over to the master, problem solver. Some things are just out of your reach: a lying tongue, a habitual gossiper, a jealous demon, a combative nature. You don't have the wherewithal to compete with any of that.

Truth is, you can confront them or even beat them up, but except God intervenes, it's a never-ending battle! Focus on God and let him focus on your reputation.

DAY 339

Do you ever examine your life and ask, What is this? Does it feel as though you were walking God along a trail; you all of a sudden slipped and fell into a dark hole, and he kept walking? You're Yelling, "Hey God!! I'm down here!" And he doesn't seem to be coming back to get you. You begin to look back over the events of your life, and you ask yourself, Did I see the hole and stepped in any way? Were there signs up along the trail, and I just ignored them? Did God know it was there and allowed me to fall in it? AM I BEING PUNKED? The answer is unknown. Yet even though you've fallen, God is still with you. No hole is too deep, and no situation is too bleak! Life is full of obstacles, but one thing you can rest in is that God is always there!

Your faith is being tried, and your relationship with him is being strengthened. GO THROUGH!! It's for your ascending, not your descending!

DAY 340

Some things in life can be a hard pill to swallow, but if you crush it and take it down slow, you'll be fine. It's not always easy, but most of the time, there's an easier way. 1. Take things day by day, 2.

Don't rush the healing process, and 3. Know that Pain doesn't last forever.

DAY 341

If you're in the midst of a storm, it's not useless. Think of it as fertilizer, Sure it feels like crap, but it will help you grow. The hardest of tests have turned out to be the greatest of victories. You can't witness to someone that "God will supply their need" unless you've experienced needing your needs met and they "in fact" were. You can't explain to someone how God will bring them out "except" you were in a situation. In the midst of someone's life tragedy, a person needs to hear your voice. 9 times out of 10, if you've not gone through this. You won't really have their attention.

Allow God to establish you so that you may be an effective witness. Someone up ahead may need to know that you made it out of the fire! It's not for naught!!

DAY 342

What works for me may not work for you, and what you like, I possibly may not like. I'm caramel in skin color, your tone may be a tad bit or a lot darker, but that doesn't make you any less beautiful. You may be a size 6, and she may be a size 22, but that doesn't make you any better than her because (to be honest) men prefer a little more meat on the bones nowadays. He may be a lawyer, and you may be a manager at McDonald's, but that doesn't mean anything because both jobs will pay the bills. The moral of this inspiration, I may not do what you do, you may not go where I go, she may not eat what you eat. He may not earn what you earn, but that's okay because God made us all different yet, we can all get along.

Don't worry about the difference. Look at how we all present something different.

DAY 343

Whether you've pushed me or pulled me, drained me, or fueled me, loved me, or hated me, hurt me, or helped me, lied or was brutally honest, cheated or was totally faithful, threw me away or kept me, put me down, or encouraged me, picked me up or dropped me like a hot potato; you are a part of my Growth, and I truly THANK YOU!!!

DAY 344

*D*on't stop the flow of your haters. Things are flowing in the order in which they should. They think they are hurting you, but in fact, they are helping. Whether it's forcing you to pray or causing you to depend on God, all things are working together to develop a greater God "in you!"

DAY 345

There are so many that would rather list you than to love you!! They have a whole list of why they hate you, another list of what you did to them, and a few other lists of things they'll do to you if you get in their way. They have no intentions of doing what's commanded, and that's to "LOVE" you. This world has turned sick, and it's sad, but people would rather go to hell than to go and get things right. There are so many that won't make it in due to pettiness.

What is more important, seeing the creator or seeing to it that you pay for what you did (or they think you did) to them? More effort should be put into fighting FOR souls ~vs. ~ AGAINST souls!! Will you list 'em or love 'em?

DAY 346

*D*o you know one of the best gifts you can give "yourself" is to love yourself!! You may hear a thousand "I love you's" in your lifetime but what drives you is the love you have for yourself. That's what keeps you going, it's what motivates you, it's what keeps you smiling in the face of adversity, as well as helps you to hold your head up while taking a long, lonely walk through a patch of Haters!

Love yourself enough that if no one ever utters those words to you, you can still make it. Nothing compares to the love you have for yourself because you know the genuineness of it,

DAY 347

Sometimes you don't want to be around people that lie all of the time. Sometimes you don't want people around that are so in love. Sometimes you don't want people around that always have a sad story. Sometimes you don't want people around that are so giddy, nor do you want someone around that is always on cloud nine. No, you're not asking for a pity party, but sometimes you just need to be alone!! Sometimes you want to ride in your car, sit in your room, or in your office ALL ALONE! You don't want to talk, laugh, or explain why you're crying. You just want to sit in silence and think. It's okay to be in solitude sometimes. That's where you can get to your inner place.

Steal away so that "not only" can you hear yourself think, but you can hear God speak!!

DAY 348

When you want to and know that "you can" go straight in on individuals, Don't!!! Honey, hold your peace!! So, what, if you know that they're broke as a joke? They (Themselves) know it too!! So, what if you know that they're perpetrators of fraud? They (Themselves) know it too!! You don't have to blast them. Pretty soon, the world will know it!! (If they don't already know) Let them continue.

Situations will open it all up without you even uttering a word! Stay classy and let the chips fall where they may!!

DAY 349

*E*verybody isn't for Everybody!! Things might not have worked with him and I, but he may be perfect for you! We've got to stop throwing shade and telling the next one all that she "Wasn't" when she was with you. She just might start doing it for HIM! (whatever the "It" is). Now, if he's choking you out (without reason), that's one thing. But if it's the mere fact that he wasn't "IN LOVE" with YOU, that doesn't mean that he won't love the snot out of HER! Don't warn me because you're jealous. Alert me because he's armed and dangerous! It could just mean I wasn't what he needed, but "THE NEXT" one could have it all in the bag and then some.

Just because this one isn't the one, make no mistake about it; God has/is making that someone that is!!

DAY 350

What seems to have a hold on you that you can't seem to break? Is it chocolate? is it soda? Shopping? Drugs/Alcohol? Is it a man/woman? What is it that keeps you going back for more? And why? Why do you not have control over this thing? A lot of times, you may say, "It's hard or I can't!" But the truth is, if you put your mind to it, you can do anything. You ever hear the cliche, mind over matter? That is so true; you keep telling yourself no! over and over! Do this consistently for about 2-3 weeks, and you'll see that it can be done. Many times, we don't overcome a thing because we're telling ourselves that we CAN'T instead of telling ourselves we CAN!

When you let a person or thing consume you, it takes away your ability to make decisions. Focus!! Keep your mind and stay in control!!

DAY 351

I teach my girls; it's an awesome thing when someone says they love you. "BUT" make sure you love yourself beforehand. "SO" if they switch up on you, you'll still be alright!!! Trust me, people are very wishy-washy at times. One day you're the next best thing to a soft piece of sliced bread (with butter), and the next, they're looking for another loaf.

Love yourself first. So, when someone else tells you, it'll add to it. There could never be too much love!!

DAY 352

Peace on the outside comes from having God on the inside. You could be going through a major disaster, yet no one knows it because you're trusting in God "inwardly" to work it out. You don't have to whine to your friends, complain to your family, or rant on social media when you're assured of God's power. Grab a hold to peace and walk through the hurricane and come out unscathed. When the Hebrew boys were thrown into the fire, not a hair on their heads was singed because They had confidence in the God they served. (Daniel 3:27) Yes, things look bad, feel bad, and may even taste bad, but once you get that peace on the inside, you can go through it without griping. Show the people around you what can be done when you just trust God!!

DAY 353

Why do we wonder "what if" ?? Just think; If "what if" was meant to be, it would be, and you wouldn't be wondering. A lot of times we live in the past by those very words "What if!" The past is called "the past" for a reason, an "Ex" is an ex for a reason, and "yesterday" was named yesterday because that was then and today is now. You're not allowing life its full potential. Your future growth is being stunted, and you're limiting yourself from "What's to come!"

Take a leap of faith into tomorrow and leave what's behind, back there!

DAY 354

*L*ife is too short to be miserable!! Make sure you're the Choice, not the option. Don't be in a relationship and still be lonely!!!

Life is too short. Be happy or be free to be happy!!! Someone is always looking for someone to love!!

DAY 355

Never make someone the H.N.I.C. when there's not even a company Don't (trust) fall unless you know they'll catch you and NEVER, and I do mean "NEVER," make them a priority when you're just merely an option!!! When you know who you are, you can be single and content until someone that recognizes your worth comes along. If you act cheap, it won't cost them anything. Some people are more apt to stay around when they feel they're losing something of value.

You're not dollar store merchandise, honey. You're Sax Fifth Avenue apparel. The very "thought" of you whispers value.

DAY 356

All sickness is not unto death, neither is every valley experience here to take you out. These tests and trials exist to strengthen you! There were times when your cupboards were bare, but you didn't starve to death. The doctors may have diagnosed you with a terminal illness, but you're here today reading this post, and perhaps you were unemployed for a while, but (guess what) your bills "STILL" got paid.

Don't focus on where you are right now. This is just a temporary situation up against a Powerful God!! Lean NOT to what it looks like; trust in what it will be!

DAY 357

It's amazing how one person can leave your life (that meant you absolutely no good, AT ALL), and it does you a world of Good! You wonder, "How did they ever become A part of my life in the first place?" How was I able to entertain them THIS LONG!?" It's like oil and water. There was never a connection. We were never compatible. Let's just face it, we were just riding the wave. Sometimes you continue with someone merely because you feel obligated or simply because you don't want to hurt their feelings, or you may feel like you're in too deep. I say life is too short to be in something uncomfortable! Rid yourself of unnecessary stress and any nonproductive relationships. It's as though you're walking around all day with vomit on your shoe (I need to wipe this off) or sitting in the living room watching tv with a plate of spoiled food on the coffee table that has been there for weeks (what's that smell?)!!

Regroup, Detach, and live in Peace!!!

DAY 358

*A*re you sleeping with the enemy?

The things you share with "friends" are they shared with someone else? Sometimes "your best friend" has a best friend, and the moment you tell them something, they're on the phone repeating it or through text revealing your business to "their best friend." What I loathe more than anything is when someone pours their heart out to someone, and it gets repeated or used later. Be careful whom you're releasing all or your treasures to. You never know what hands they're going to end up in. Stop and ask yourself, "Is this person mature enough to handle the magnitude of this news?" The truth is some people just don't know how to handle or know what to do with all that you dumped on them. So, they run and tell someone else.

Before you trust, you'd better trace their past safe keepings.

DAY 359

The devil will take you further than you want to go, keep you longer than you want to stay And then leave you there to die! Don't trust him. HE IS NOT YOUR FRIEND!! No matter how appealing things may look, the end result will always be bad!! Yeah, it feels good to turn up, cuss out, commit adultery/fornicate, etc. But nothing beats walking in righteousness. The enemy is slick, cunning, and some mo' things. He will have you thinking that wrong is right and right is wrong! Be careful what you do because "that smooth joker" will talk you into it then expose you!!

Wait on the hand of God. And follow God's lead ONLY!!!!

DAY 360

*L*isten, before you talk about someone, make sure you're perfect. Make sure you have no spots or blemishes. REMEMBER; just because you call her fat, it doesn't make you skinny. Just because you say he's ugly, that sure doesn't make you handsome. TRUTH IS we ALL have something in us, on us and with us that we are not so fond of, and Gossip can go both ways. There's nothing worse (to me) than a Gossiping "Grown" Woman or MAN!!! And yesss, Men Gossip too!!!!! If you don't like their mole, IT'S NOT YOURS!! We have to learn to keep our opinions to ourselves. I might not like someone, but the next woman might LOVE him!! What's not for you may be perfect for someone else.

When you're paying YOUR OWN hard-earned money for it, Unless I put in on it, "MY" input is not needed. Ride quietly or get out!!

DAY 361

The diversity "OF" life has made you who you are today!!! There have been ups, downs, good days, and days that felt like a nightmare! The tough days showed you your strength, and when the great days rolled around, you were able to appreciate them. This thing can be compared to that of a see-saw. You can be wonderful one day and horrible the next, but all of it combined creates balance. Even the prettiest of rose has thorns, so with every trial comes experience. Although it may not feel good, it benefits you because you're much more the wiser.

Let life run its course - the good, the bad, the ups "AND" the downs. A greater you is in production!!

DAY 362

If you're broken, tell God. If you're weak, tell God; if you have a problem, admit it. Whatever you're going through, God can heal and deliver you. Holding it in isn't the key. Suicide isn't the way, and a lot of times, telling others doesn't help.

Find you an altar and lay it all at his feet. He's waiting to carry you through.

DAY 363

You know what would create a world of peace? If we'd learn how to get things right with one another instead of holding grudges!! Also, if one would express their hurts to someone you've felt hurt you, instead of involving others. We spread the fire by adding more people to the equation. Life is extremely short. It is vitally important that we release anything that could potentially hinder us from making it in. It's a dangerous thing to know what is detrimental to life eternal and continue in those areas.

NOTHING is more important than Peace!! Stop the madness and live a life of purpose, not in bitterness.

DAY 364

*S*ingle ladies: The longer you are single, the more "your Value" increases. (Remember, the longer wine sits, the better it gets!!!) Use this time "not" to whine & complain; utilize this time to augment your worth!! So, when he comes, you won't accept any ole' thang, and HE wouldn't have FOUND any ole' thang!!!

DAY 365

There is nothing you need to do to deserve happiness. There are no 'minimal requirements' for you to fulfill, no long list of People to impress, no backs to stab even!!

You deserve happiness simply by virtue of being God's Child!! That's it!! Nothing more is required. #Be happy

ABOUT THE AUTHOR

Daphanny Denette C. Baker is a native of Plant City, Fla.. but was Raised in Newark, NJ. She Graduated from Ewing High School in Trenton, NJ.

She soon went on to pursue a career in Cosmetology, where she obtained her license. She later took an interest in the corrections field and acquired a bachelor's degree in Criminal Justice; She is presently working on her Master's in Business Administration.

Daphanny is a Worship leader; she also devotes much of her time using her "scarred hands" to help hurting individuals. She's a Wife, a Mother of 4, and the First Lady of her local Assembly.

facebook.com/daphanny.baker
twitter.com/daphdiva1
instagram.com/daphannybaker

www.ingramcontent.com/pod-product-compliance
Lightning Source LLC
Chambersburg PA
CBHW071953110526
44592CB00012B/1074